D1499848

The Surveillance of Women
on Reality Television

Critical Studies in Television

SERIES EDITOR

Mark Andrejevic, University of Iowa

ADVISORY BOARD

Robin Andersen, Fordham University

Lynn Schofield Clark, University of Denver

James Hay, University of Illinois at Urbana-Champaign

Fred Turner, Stanford University

This series critically examines television, emphasizing in-depth monographic studies on a particular television series. By looking at television through a critical lens, the books in this series will bring insight into the cultural significance of television, and also explore how the lessons apply to larger critical and social issues. The texts in the series will appeal to communication, media, and cultural theory scholars.

Titles in Series:

Dawson's Creek: A Critical Understanding by Lori Bindig

Dear Angela: Remembering My So-Called Life edited by Michele Byers and David Lavery

Tribal Warfare: Survivor *and the Political Unconscious of Reality Television* by Christopher J. Wright

The CSI *Effect: Television, Crime, and Governance* edited by Michele Byers and Val Marie Johnson

Popular Culture and the Future of Politics: Cultural Studies and the Tao of South Park by Ted Gournelos

The Surveillance of Women on Reality Television: Watching The Bachelor *and* The Bachelorette by Rachel E. Dubrofsky

The Surveillance of Women on Reality Television

Watching *The Bachelor* and *The Bachelorette*

Rachel E. Dubrofsky

LEXINGTON BOOKS
Lanham • Boulder • New York • Toronto • Plymouth, UK

Published by Lexington Books
A wholly owned subsidary of The Rowman & Littlefield Publishing Group, Inc.
4501 Forbes Boulevard, Suite 200, Lanham, Maryland 20706
http://www.lexingtonbooks.com

Estover Road, Plymouth PL6 7PY, United Kingdom

An earlier version of Chapter 2 appeared as "The Bachelor: Whiteness in the Harem" by Rachel E. Dubrofsky in *Critical Studies in Media Communication*, 23(1), 2006 by Taylor & Francis Ltd.. Reprinted by permission of Taylor & Francis Ltd, http://www.informaworld.com.

An earlier version of Chapter 4 appeared as "Fallen Women on Reality TV: A Pornography of Emotion" by Rachel E. Dubrofsky in *Feminist Media Studies*, 9(3), 2009 by Taylor & Francis Ltd.. Reprinted by permission of Taylor & Francis Ltd, http://www.informaworld.com.

An earlier version of Chapter 5 appeared as "'Therapeutics of the Self': Surveillance in the Service of the Therapeutic" in *Television and New Media*, 8(4) by SAGE Publications Ltd., All rights reserved. © 2007. http://online.sagepub.com/

British Library Cataloguing in Publication Information Available

Library of Congress Cataloging-in-Publication Data
Dubrofsky, Rachel E.
  The surveillance of women on reality television : watching The bachelor and The bachelorette / Rachel E. Dubrofsky.
    p. cm. — (Critical studies in television)
  Includes bibliographical references and index.
  ISBN 978-0-7391-6498-3 (cloth : alk. paper)
  1. Reality television programs—Social aspects. 2. Women on television. 3. Bachelor (Television program) 4. Bachelorette (Television program) I. Title.
  PN1992.8.R43D73 2011
  791.45'655—dc22   2011008407

Printed in the United States of America

To my two favorite people, my mom and my little sister.

Table of Contents

Acknowledgments

Many people influenced and shaped this project, supporting me and my work. It is an honor to count among my biggest supporters Kent A. Ono, chair of my dissertation (the basis of the book) committee and steadfast mentor ever since. The pages of this book are an expression of his guidance. He is a rambunctious cheerleader at all times. Without his unending intellectual input, enthusiasm (even when mine lagged), and ongoing support, this project would never have been realized.

I am thankful to the Institute of Communications Research at the University of Illinois, Urbana-Champaign, for providing a safe haven for those of us who do critical cultural studies work and for bringing me into contact with so many inspiring scholars. I am grateful to Sarah Projansky for committing to this project at a time when it was not easy for her to do so and continually appreciative of her wonderfully intelligent insights that surprise and push my thinking in new directions. Sarah is a steady source of encouragement, sure to convey her excitement about my work and show me its strengths. In the early stages, Paula A. Treichler's attention to detail, to the particularities of insightful analysis, and to the nuances of words deepened my understanding of my own work and helped me reveal it in my writing. I am forever indebted to her for making sure I was able to do this project on my own terms. James Hay's dedication to this project provided guidance and direction. I am especially grateful for our café meetings where we discussed television and Foucault. Angharad N. Valdivia kindly and generously directed me to much needed resources at a particularly crucial moment in my research. John Nerone is my superhero, there when I needed him to swoop in and save the day. I am truly indebted to him.

Susan J. Harewood, Diem-My T. Bui, and Paul Luu generously shared their insights and experiences, patiently standing by me as I stumbled my way toward gaining insight and perspective on issues of race. Many of these Chapters would not have been written without Susan's always clear, spot-on, and witty insights. Countless times she provided the missing link, reminding me of what I was trying to do (and why it was important). I am also grateful to Susan for being my family while in Champaign-Urbana. I am thankful for Craig Robertson, with his endearingly dark sense of humor, incredibly analytical mind, and curmudgeonly way of always being supportive and encouraging.

Joan Chan, Victor Mendoza, Ellen McWhorter, Shoshana Magnet, and Robert Smith brightened up the last months of dissertating in Champaign-Urbana with good company and laughter. I am thankful for Carrie Rentschler, a constant advocate and someone who provided wonderful insights on early drafts of parts of this work.

At the University of South Florida, in the Department of Communication, Kenneth Cissna has been a supportive and generous chair through the different stages of this project. Arthur Bochner, who I consider my mentor in the department, is always supportive and ready to offer guidance. I am thankful to the department for giving me Blake Paxton, my dear research assistant for the last leg of this journey, efficient, patient, wonderfully on top of things and good-humored.

From the very beginning, Mark Andrejevic's scholarship provided an amazing jumping-off point for this work. Mark was a generous and supportive series editor, selecting this book and fighting to make sure it was published in a manner that would preserve the integrity of the work. I am indebted to Linda Steiner, who put me through writing boot-camp when, as the editor of *Critical Studies in Media Communication*, she diligently helped me edit an article published in 2006 that was the basis of Chapter 2 of this book. This experience taught me much of what I know about getting something ready for publication. I am also thankful to Rebecca J. McCary at Lexington Books for coming through at a crucial time to make sure this book made it to publication.

In Tampa, I am blessed to have as dear friends Warren L. Rose, who reminds me, always, that life is full of adventure, and Melanie Berios, who keeps me sane in body and mind and who is always full of wonderful surprises. Grateful also for Julie Alexander, who has taught me how to have a good time no matter what. Happy to count Penny Carlton among my friends, for her gentle insight and wisdom, always, Tony Adams, who burst into my life with his insane giggles, showing me the best spots in our hood, and Lucas Mehl for sweet fun times. I am thankful for Mariaelena Bartesaghi, whose nuggets of witty insight are worth more than I can say, and to Asmaa Malik for her friendship and delight in my work. I am always grateful for my dearest childhood friends, Kim Brand and T'Cha Dunlevy, who made the "getting on" with the work that much easier by reminding me that there is a world of fun and adventure beyond this project.

I am honored by the presence of my little sister, Seiyan Yang, who, already at her young age when I began this project, taught me about courage, determination, and grace as she navigated the many obstacles in her own life and accomplished incredible feats. She inspired me to complete this project, not only so I could be a role model of sorts for her but so she would know how much I have learned from her. Her goofy and sweet spirit fills my life with warmth.

Finally, words cannot express how grateful I am to my mother, Debby Dubrofsky. Although she did not let me watch TV when I was young, it was she who ordered me to watch the first episode of *Survivor*, insisting it would be important for my research. She could not have been more correct. Her mark is on every single page of this work, due to her careful and painstaking editing, countless insights, and unending support. She was proud of me throughout the process and a constant source of encouragement. I am incredibly blessed to have her as my mother.

surveillance technologies
racialized/gendered
bodies

Introduction: The "Bachelor Industry"

Since the phenomenal success of *Survivor* in the summer of 2000, reality TV has become a staple of prime-time programming. *The Bachelor*, the focus of this book, is the most successful reality romance show to date and one of the most successful reality TV shows of all time. ABC aired the first season of *The Bachelor* in March 2002. At the time of this writing, the fourteenth season recently ended, a fifteenth is in the works (to air in January 2011), and the sixth season of its spin-off, *The Bachelorette*, recently aired, as did the first season of a new spin-off, *Bachelor Pad*. One of the first in the contemporary reality genre (shows like *Real World, Survivor, Big Brother*), *The Bachelor* is the most enduring reality romance show in a genre characterized by short-lived programming.

Season after season, week after week, *The Bachelor* has brought us "the most shocking rose ceremony ever" and created a virtual industry of ideas about reality, surveillance, authenticity, women, and love. This work is the first book-length feminist analysis of the reality TV phenomena and the first to focus on a single series and its spin-off. It asks us to think about how the call to the real, on which reality TV relies, configures representations of women on television. For instance, what happens when we can say "but she really was that hysterical and out-of-control—we saw it" as opposed to "why did the writers and producers of the series create another hysterical and out-of-control female character?"

An important part of the conversation about women on reality TV is the role of surveillance in this setup. The use of surveillance technologies, coupled with the use of real people (nonactors), raises questions about representations of the real and the authentic on television, which can have particular implications for gendered and racialized bodies. In this work, I ask: How are racialized and gendered bodies produced by surveillance in the space of reality TV? In what ways are requirements for authentic behavior gendered and raced in this context? What are the implications of a call to the real for certain bodies in this space?

1

Symptomatic Texts

(1)

While the focus is on the long-running reality TV series *The Bachelor* as a lens for my discussion, I also look at its spin-off, *The Bachelorette*. I have always enjoyed watching these shows. They entertain and fascinate. They are also perplexing. This push-and-pull is a fruitful standpoint from which to begin a critical analysis, allowing for respect and understanding for the craft that goes into creating a popular media product and a questioning of why things appear as they do in the shows. Since I am interested primarily in how women are configured in the space of reality TV, *The Bachelorette*, with only one woman (as the star), provides less material for fruitful analysis. These texts are my reflective sites of inquiry. I view the shows as what Walters (1995) calls "symptomatic texts" (p. 6), that is, texts that alert us of a cultural moment in process rather than a moment from whence certain things begin to happen. I examine the texts as symptoms of the condition of the culture in which they exist (Walters, 1995, p. 10), as articulating discourses at work and illustrating how these function. For instance, Walters (1995) suggests that the film *Fatal Attraction* (Lyne, 1987) signaled the emergence of postfeminist representations of the dangers for women who mistakenly chose career over family (p. 123). *Fatal Attraction* was one popular media text, among many at that particular time, displaying these issues. By analyzing this particular film, we are able to articulate some of the cultural anxieties about women entering the workforce and taking on challenging careers, as well as the fears about how these actions by women would impact family life. Symptomatic texts provide clues to the nature of the larger cultural context in which they emerge.

I am committed to seeing cultural phenomena as particular, contingent, and contextual. With an intense focus on, and sustained analysis of, the mechanisms and the workings of discourses in a specific media space, I can access an understanding of how things come to "make sense," how they function in that space, thus opening up discussions of how these same discourses, and other related ones, function in other media spaces. I am invested in the details of how things work on these shows, not because I am specifically interested in these shows (though I do enjoy them and believe this is a necessary precondition to studying a media text) but because the shows engage circulating discourses about gender. I am invested in the intersection of surveillance and gendered bodies in popular media sites and in exploring the productivity of this intersection. As a result, I do not examine the media amplification of the texts surrounding *The Bachelor* and *The Bachelorette* (appearances by participants on other television shows, interviews with participants, and so forth),[1] nor do I look at other reality TV shows, television shows, or audience responses to the shows. Instead, I examine the media texts on their own turf, dissecting the terms of the shows, exploring how the shows invite audiences to view them and to think about gender and race, and scrutinizing the role of surveillance in this setup.

Women and Romance: Failing at Love

What makes the two series, *The Bachelor* and *The Bachelorette*, pertinent for an analysis of women in popular media is their focus on romance, which keys into many popular discourses about women and attracts a female audience. These are texts about women, for women. While men may be the stars of each season of *The Bachelor*, they are not, in fact, given much screen time: the women are. Anyone who has watched the show knows that the women are the most memorable characters, not the men. Hysterical or emotional women are front and center. There is an inherent paradox in the setup of the show: while the explicit premise is to help two people find love, the action of the series revolves around women who are unable to win the love of the bachelor, propelled by a drawn-out process of eliminating unsuitable women until all but one remains. The narrative focuses on how and why women are *not* selected, with the most screen time devoted to these women. In many seasons, even the woman who wins the bachelor's heart is not central (given significant screen time) until the last few episodes, and sometimes not even until the final episode. Her behavior is usually quite staid, with few emotional outbursts, and her emotionality is never cast as excessive, as it is for the women who take center stage during the season. In fact, *The Bachelor* does not tell a story about love, about a couple coming together to find love; rather it is a tale of the treacherous journey of women who fail at love. This may explain why *The Bachelor* is a far more successful TV product than *The Bachelorette* (evidenced by the number of seasons of *The Bachelor* compared to *The Bachelorette*): it puts on display women who fail at love. It may also explain why only one of the couples from the fourteen seasons of *The Bachelor* remain together and are married at the time of this writing, season thirteen's Jason Mesnick and Molly Malaney (though Molly was actually the second runner-up and not the woman Jason initially chose at the end of the season). Most of the other couples broke up within a few months of the finale of the series, with a few couples dating for several years, such as Byron Velvick and Mary Delgado from season six (together for five years), and Charlie O'Connell and Sarah Brice from season seven (they dated on and off for about four years). Odds are slightly better for the six seasons of *The Bachelorette* (where the focus is not on women who fail at love), with, at the time of this writing, one marriage (Trista Rhen and Ryan Sutter from season one), and one engagement (Ali Fedotowsky and Roberto Martinez from season six).

The focus on failed love in *The Bachelor* is similar to what Janice Radway describes as central to the romance novel in her influential work *Reading the Romance* (1984). Radway posits that the core of the romance novel is the heroine's ability to overcome her original resistance to a man and see him for who he really is: a suitable romantic partner. She argues this is a story about the refashioning, or feminization, of the overly masculine man to conform to the conceptions of masculinity that women desire. Conversely, the core of the narrative in *The Bachelor* is the hero's ability to overcome his original attraction to a woman and see her for who she "really" is: an *un*suitable romantic partner. Once he is able to do this, he can turn his attentions to a more suitable romantic partner. As in the novels Radway examines, it is the women (not the men) who are the heart of the story. While reveling in showing women who fail at love is not a novel story on television, the call to the real through the filming of real people under surveillance adds a new twist.

Ratings *premise*

The Bachelor and *The Bachelorette* are impressive prime-time events for a major network like ABC. With the first season garnering an average 11.9 million viewers (Lisotta, April 18, 2005, pp. 10-11), *TV Guide* declared *The Bachelor* "ABC's Most Valuable Player" (*TV Guide*, September 7-13, 2002, p. 36). The show put ABC back on the ratings map, knocking NBC's *The West Wing* out of first place in the key 18-49 demographic (Collins, October 11-13, 2002, p. 1), the most lucrative TV slot and demographic. The second season showed a significant increase in viewers with an average 16.7 million (Lisotta, April 18, 2005, pp. 10-11). In this industry the success of the second season is especially significant, as it "separates true hits from also-rans" (Collins, November 6, 2002, p. 4). This success had tangible long-term benefits for ABC, which recorded the biggest growth in viewers in the fall of 2002, when it aired the second season (Collins, December 4, 2002, p. 31). Since then, ratings for *The Bachelor* have been respectable but inconsistent over the seasons. Season three averaged 12.6 million viewers, and season four 13.6 million viewers (Rogers, April 28, 2004). The "After the Final Rose" episode for season four, which reunited the bachelor from season four and his chosen woman, beat out the consistent ratings heavy-hitter *Survivor: Pearl Islands* in its time slot, stealing away two million viewers (Rogers, October 22, 2003). Season five averaged 11.2 million viewers, season six 8.8 million viewers, season seven 7.9 million viewers, season eight 9.3 million (Azote, March 8, 2006). The first five episodes of season nine averaged 8.06 million viewers (Rogers, November 17, 2006). The finale for season ten fared well, attracting 12.7 million viewers (Maynard, May 31, 2007, p. C07). The season finale for season eleven won over 11.2 million viewers, and the "After the Final Rose" episode fared even better with 12.3 million viewers (Levin, p. 3D, November 28, 2007). The finale for season twelve did not do so well with only 8.5 million viewers tuning in (de Moraes, May 21, 2008, p. C01), but the series was renewed for a thirteenth season, which had a 37 percent increase in ratings over season twelve (Adalian, February 11, 2009). Season thirteen averaged 10.4 million viewers (Adalian, February 11, 2009). This season, "the show has been growing week-to-week since it premiered in early January—the first 'Bachelor' to do so since 2003. And among its target audience of young women, the latest 'Bachelor' stands as the no. 6 show on TV among females 18-34" (February 11, 2009). For season fourteen, the series garnered an average 12.0 million viewers (Mika, March 10, 2010). Season fourteen's "After the Final Rose" episode won over 14.3 million viewers (Mika, March 10, 2010). As Azote (March 8, 2006) remarked early on, which still holds true, while ratings for *The Bachelor* have ebbed and flowed, it remains "a strategic component of ABC's schedule."

The first season of *The Bachelorette* aired in January 2003 and was a ratings hit, with an average 16.7 million viewers. The final episode of the three-part special "Trista and Ryan's Wedding" (the wedding of the bachelorette and her chosen man) won the time slot for the evening with 17.1 million viewers (Rogers, December 13, 2003). The second season of *The Bachelorette* showed a decline in ratings, with an average 11.5 million viewers. The third season fared worst, with an average 8.6 million viewers (Lisotta, April 18, 2005, pp. 10-11). However, the show was renewed for a fourth season, the finale of which won ABC the top spot for the evening, attracting 9.5 million viewers. The "After the Final Rose" episode for season four won over 10 million viewers (Toff, July 9, 2008). Season five averaged 8.1 million viewers per week, the finale drawing 9.9 million (Kaufman, July 28, 2009). For season six, Seidman (July 20, 2010) reports that "On average . . . 'The Bachelorette' was up over the previous year (season five) by 1.6 million viewers (9.8 million vs. 8.2 million)." This season was the most watched since 2004 (Seidman, July 20, 2010). The sixth season finale had ABC finishing number one in the time period for a tenth consecutive week, surpassing CBS by 5 million viewers (Seidman, July 20, 2010).

To give an idea of what this means in monetary terms, according to an article on Forbes online, *The Bachelor* and *The Bachelorette* were among the top five most profitable U.S. reality TV shows at the height of their early popularity in 2004, with *The Bachelor* pulling in a network profit of $38.2 million for the fourth season (with a price tag of $231,400 per thirty-second advertising spot), and *The Bachelorette* pulling in a network profit of $27.7 million for the second season (with a price tag of $178,000 per thirty-second advertising spot) (Patsuris, September 7, 2004).

The Shows   *premix*

Some details about the shows provide background information for the arguments in this book. Each season of *The Bachelor* has a man (a different one each season) select from among twenty-five eligible women, over an eight-week period, one woman to be his potential wife. Most episodes last between an hour and two hours (increasingly in later seasons the trend has been for episodes lasting two hours). There are a total of ten episodes a season (including "The Women Tell All" and the "After the Final Rose" episodes), with a few exceptions (for instance, season thirteen had a two-part "After the Final Rose" episode). The main action of the series revolves around the bachelor whittling down an original pool of twenty-five eligible women to his final selection. This varies on a few seasons. In two seasons of *The Bachelor*, for instance, a few women (one or two) are added in the middle of the season. Typically, there is a rose ceremony at the end of each episode in which the bachelor offers a rose to each of the participants he wants to remain on the show. As the seasons progressed, however, the series incorporated new ways of eliminating participants in addition to the ceremonies, such as "elimination dates" where two people go on a date with the star of the series but only one returns (the other is sent home at the end of the date). On *The Bachelorette*, the format is the same, except that the star of the series is a woman and she picks one man out of twenty-five eligible bachelors to be her potential husband (exceptionally, five additional men are added to the pool in the first episode of season five). She offers the men rose boutonnières instead of long-stemmed roses at the ceremonies. Even though the roles are reversed, with the woman picking the men and much vaunting of the fact that a woman is in the driver's seat, the series follows the same normative gender prescriptions and expectations as *The Bachelor*. For instance, on *The Bachelorette* it is up to the final chosen man to propose to the bachelorette at the end of the season (the women never propose to the men).

Between rose ceremonies, participants go on group dates with the star, and a lucky few go on individual dates. Participants can choose to leave the show at the ceremony (or at any other point), regardless of what the star may decide. The elimination process follows a general pattern, with some variation: the first week the star narrows the group from twenty-five to fifteen, the second week from fifteen to twelve, the third week from ten to eight, the fourth week from eight to six, the fifth week down to four, the sixth week to three, the seventh week to two, and then the final selection is made. When the star narrows the pool to three or four, each remaining participant brings the star home to meet family and friends. The star has the opportunity to go on individual overnight dates, which generally happen when there are three remaining participants. The series implies that participants share physical intimacy during these dates, and though the possibility for sexual intercourse is present, we are not given confirmation about what takes place. In the finale of the series, or in the episode prior, the star invites the remaining two participants to his or her hometown to meet the family, or the family is flown to the location where the series is being filmed to meet the star's prospective mates. On this episode, the star of *The Bachelor*, or the male participants on *The Bachelorette*, purchase an engagement ring to propose (or to offer other levels of commitment) once the final selection is made. The men can offer the ring as a promise for a potential future together, hold onto it for possible future engagement, or offer it as an engagement ring.

About two episodes per season are taped in talk-show format. On most seasons, when only two participants remain, an episode entitled "The Women Tell All" or "The Men Tell All" airs in which many of the eliminated participants gather in a studio with an audience and host Chris Harrison to discuss their experiences. At the end of most seasons, an episode entitled "After the Final Rose" airs, which is also filmed in front of a live studio audience.

In addition to the shows that make up the season, there are occasional specials. For instance, there was the three-part special "Trista and Ryan's Wedding," which showed the wedding preparations and the wedding of Trista, star of the first season of *The Bachelorette* and her chosen man Ryan. The same was done in the special "Molly and Jason's Wedding" (only one episode though) for the star of the thirteenth season of *The Bachelor*, Jason, and the woman he marries, Molly (the second runner-up—he breaks up with his final chosen woman).

The shows have evolved over time, keeping audiences on their toes by mixing things up when it comes to the expected format of the series. For example, the elimination process was tinkered with to add elements of the unexpected: in early seasons, participants were selected and eliminated only at rose ceremonies, but in later seasons new ways of selecting and eliminating participants were added—such as the "first impression rose," where the star, on the first episode, prior to the elimination ceremony, offers a rose to the participant who made the best first impression (thereby inviting the person to remain on the show). In addition, increasingly as the seasons progressed, the stars began to step outside the elimination process as set up by the series. For instance, Jake Pavelka, star of season fourteen of *The Bachelor*, eliminates both women on an elimination date—instead of just one, as the makers of the show had arranged. Over time, participants (and viewers) who have watched previous seasons come to know the routine of the series. To reflect this, makers of the show increasingly include moments when participants jokingly comment on the action by saying things like "is this the hot tub scene?" referencing the ubiquitous scenes in hot tubs featured on every season. An awareness on the part of the makers of the show that audiences would come to find these scenes predictable prompted the inclusion of self-referencing moments.

The Bachelor Industry: Making Sense of Things

As outlined above, the first season of *The Bachelor* started a financially success-ful television series that set the stage for a virtual "Bachelor Industry" (hereafter BI), a term I use to describe the larger television event that includes fourteen seasons (and counting) of *The Bachelor*, six seasons of *The Bachelorette* (and counting), and many related program specials in the United States.[2] The "BI" is a convenient phrase, allowing me to discuss all shows related to *The Bachelor* at once.[3] However, I also push the boundaries of a political economic understanding of the term "industry" (as exemplified in the work of McChesney, 1999; Schiller, 1999; and Wasco, 2002) by insisting that analyzing a television industry can mean looking beyond the typical factors of a political economy perspective—the economic and policy aspects of producing a television show—to an investigation of the delimitations of a particular industry (here defined as the two series), the space the industry constructs, the ideas promoted, the implications, and the mechanisms used to create these things.

My take on the BI insists that to make sense of it we need an arsenal of tools and perspectives. In this way, the book cuts across a perspective that would use a genre studies framework, or a surveillance studies one, or a romance and gender one, or a critical race studies one, instead bringing all of these areas of scholarship into conversation in the service of understanding the critical implications of the BI.

My approach underlines the need to question the logic that makes things appear real, authentic, rational, and necessary. While the terms "real" and "authentic" are not put in quotation marks throughout the work, they should be understood as such, since the work assumes that notions of the real and the authentic are unstable, contingent, and contextual: there is no essential authentic or real that underlies what we see on television. Rather, the book explores the production, sustenance, and technologizing of ideas (especially about the real and the authentic) and dynamics as they come to make sense in a specific and contingent context, revealing my Foucauldian affiliations. Foucault (1995) looks at the ways in which institutions produce certain types of behavior, and how these come into being. For instance, he examines how prisons produce docile bodies, bodies that obey the rules of the prison and are thus ideal inhabitants of that institution (Foucault, 1995). To illustrate this idea, Foucault (1995) uses Bentham's panopticon, a prison organized around a central tower from which a guard can see into every cell (though the prisoners cannot see into the tower). The prisoners thus discipline their behavior based on the fear of being watched, regardless of whether the guard in the tower is actually watching them. The disciplining is therefore noncoercive, individuals regulating themselves to be the right kind of citizen based on the requirements of the institution. I use this approach to analyze the space of the BI and the behavior of its inhabitants.

I also take my cue from Grossberg (1997), who articulates the aim of cultural studies as primarily antihumanistic, that is, as working against any sense of essentialist humanness. He implores us to look at what emerges for subjects "placed in real and overdetermined historical realities" (p. 240). Most importantly, he argues for a practice that does not see the qualities that make us human as intrinsic, for one that focuses on how "our practices produce our identity and our humanity, often behind our backs" (p. 240). Thus, while

> Antihumanism does not deny individuality, subjectivity, experience, or agency; it simply historicizes and politicizes them, their construction, and their relationships. If there is no essential human nature, we are always struggling to produce its boundaries, to constitute an effective (and hence real) human nature, but one that is different in different social formations. (Grossberg, 1997, p. 241)

Taking my cue from Foucault and Grossberg, I look at how the practices in the BI are produced, created, and emerge out of a certain logic, and key into circulating discourses in Western culture. I also explore how the space of the BI privileges some practices above others, forefronting that these are not the culmination of a "natural" inclination but rather "one option among many" (Gauntlett, 2002, p. 128). The logic on the shows require an entire industry to make it "make sense": the BI. I locate "accretions of techniques formed into a logical and systematic whole" (Kendall and Wickham, 2001, p. 150) that form the BI. I look at the process of verification, that is, as Robertson suggests (2006, 2009), the practices and procedures that authenticate and authorize things. In this way, the practice of verification produces a verifiable object (Robertson, 2006, 2009), and involves pulling apart the implicit rules for how we are supposed to do something (Foucault, 1988; Foucault, 1991, p. 75; Bennett, 2003, p. 47). In this case, "the ways in which people put forward, and police, their 'selves' in society; and the ways in which available discourses may enable or discourage various practices of the self" (Gauntlett, 2002, p. 125). In the BI, this means examining how ideas about authentic and real people are produced, how these are privileged or discouraged. This book looks at what makes for an "ideal" citizen in the space of the BI, and what makes for a less than ideal one, pulling apart what are constructed as essential virtues for the women, pinpointing how the women's behaviors come to make sense within the specific space of the BI, thus highlighting the parameters and requirements of that space and ultimately denaturalizing ideas about gender that emerge in this context.

In discussing the method he uses to identify "reality" and "rationality" within a given textual universe, Foucault writes that he

> isn't assessing things in terms of an absolute against which they could be evaluated as constituting more or less perfect forms of rationality, but rather examining how forms of rationality inscribe themselves in practices or systems of practices, and what role they play within them, because it's true that 'practices' don't exist without a certain regime of rationality. (Foucault, 1991, p. 79)

It takes an entire system to produce "rationality," and this rationality only makes sense (is rational) within that system. Using a different system, we might discover that "things 'weren't as necessary as all that'" (Foucault, 1991, p. 76). My work asks why, in the BI (and, by extension, in U.S. culture), things are "as necessary as all that" when it comes to women. This is an explicit move away from seeing behavior as emerging naturally, as expressing an essential quality about human nature or about an individual. The aim, instead, is to explore and unravel the requirements involved in making things appear as they are.

what is natural/
rational
is only that
w/ in the universe
created w/i
by BI

Reality TV

In scripted shows, what we might call the "real" relies on the reproduction and representation of characters, events, and scenarios that viewers can recognize as possible in the lived world. As will be discussed in Chapter 4, in scripted shows there is no call to the real in the way there is on a reality TV show but rather an attempt to reproduce events, characters, and actions that represent the real in ways that are familiar, or that create contexts in which characters can experience things and feel emotions in ways that seem familiar—as if they could happen in that way in the lived world (fantastical and fantasy elements notwithstanding). Reality TV is a different kind of beast, not only maintaining but formally emphasizing (through the formal elements, the ways in which the show is put together) the desire to show the real.

I use the term "reality TV" to refer to unscripted shows, although most have a very specific structure (with set tasks and events for each episode). Many shows that fall into this category have story editors. Thus, it might be more accurate to say that the term "reality TV" refers to shows in which editors use unscripted scenes (which are often carefully crafted and contrived) to create storylines that generally involve people who are not professional actors—except, for instance, in shows such as *The Surreal Life*, where a group of B-list actors and celebrities are filmed living together for a few weeks. The twist on reality TV shows, unlike in scripted shows, is that the actions of real people make up the fictional action of the text. Mike Fleiss, creator-executive producer of *The Bachelor*

admits that his show is a triumph of condensation. "We shot 700 hours to get six hours of television for 'The Bachelor.'" He recalls "A seven-hour date might seem boring when you tape it. But once you boil it down to seven minutes, it starts to seem like there were all sorts of fireworks going on." (Richmond, July 8, 2002, p. 21)

An important premise of reality TV is that producers cannot use anything participants did not give them (by enacting it on film). Thus, the raw material that creates a reality TV product is infused with the real actions of real people. And so, in the space of a reality TV show, a call to the real—real people, real footage—is integral. The realness is rooted in an understanding that the footage that creates the television product stems from the observation of real people captured on film. However, to some extent, the action on reality TV shows is a fiction that produces fictional characters, like the action on scripted shows. This book assumes that whatever we see on the show is a narrative put together by producers and editors from a tiny percentage of the miles of footage shot. I take film scholar Stam's (1991) approach to the study of screen media and see characters in reality TV shows "not as 'real' people, but rather as discursive constructions" (p. 253). The production process (editing, camera work, mise-en-scène) involved in putting together an episode of a reality TV show makes these television texts, and the representations of participants, constructed fictions. The final television text could have been an entirely different product depending on the footage selected and the editing process. Kraszewski (2004) sums up this process in his analysis of the representation of race on *The Real World*: "producers selected potential elements of racial conflict and misunderstanding, setting up possible versions of reality for the show. Editing also shaped the reality of the issue" (p. 180). The story about race on *The Real World* came into being through the editing process, which was guided by a particular version of what racial conflict should look like on the series and governed by a specific model of reality with certain rules of logic.

The "production relationship" is inversed in reality TV compared to scripted shows: the cast directs the producers to the extent that the cast provides the raw material producers work with to create a story, rather than producers relying on the cast to realize a scripted story. But the work that goes into casting, editing, and creating scenarios for participants to navigate belies the hand producers have in shaping the story throughout the process. The work that goes into creating the final product—the reality TV show—is often obfuscated. Unraveling this process, making clear that the images are mediated, is a necessary part of delineating the implications of the representations of gendered and racialized identity and the power relations produced in the space of a reality TV show. Toward this end, I look at how things are constructed within a given context that has a particular logic, and, as Stam (1991) notes of film analysis, this shifts "attention from the question of realism and positive and negative characters to one of voices and discourses. What were the 'accents' and 'intonations,' to use Bahktinian language, discernible in a filmic voice?" (p. 255) and specifically, "which of the ambient ethnic voices are 'heard' in a film and which are elided or distorted?" (Stam, 1991, p. 255). An underlying question in this work is: what mechanisms are set in motion in the BI to make certain voices heard in specific ways?

A Brief History: Reality Romance Shows

The history of the reality TV genre and its roots is complicated. Scholars include different types of shows under the category "reality TV." In addition to the contemporary form of reality TV shows (beginning with *Real World* and including shows like *Survivor*, *Big Brother*, and *American Idol*), scholars sometimes include talk shows, game shows, or both. While this book is interested in the contemporary genre, and specifically in the subset of shows that center on the filming of real people over time with the aim of developing a narrative about their activities segmented into serial episodes, I recognize that the scope of shows included in the term "reality TV" exceeds this focus.

Briefly, the roots of reality TV go back to August 1948, when ABC first aired *Candid Camera* (Andrejevic, 2004, p. 91; Clissold, 2004, p. 33), a program showing ordinary people unsuspectingly filmed in outrageous situations staged by the producers of the show. Reality TV, in the broadest sense of the term, has been around for over five decades. However, the first televised "sneak-peak" into the lives of ordinary people over an extended period of time, allowing for the development of a narrative over a stretch of time (and its airing in serial segments) did not appear until 1973, when PBS aired *An American Family*, a documentary series about the Loud family, who let cameras observe their lives for seven months. In 1992, in an attempt to update the format of *An American Family*, MTV aired *The Real World* (Andrejevic, 2004, p. 72), which is still on the air and represents the first contemporary reality TV show. The series, which places eight strangers in a house to live together and films their every move, is perhaps the prototype for the contemporary narrative-driven reality TV genre. First aired in 2000 on CBS and still on the air, *Survivor* was an instant hit and marked the beginning of the period when contemporary reality TV became an integral and essential part of prime-time programming schedules.

Reality shows that focus on romance have been on the air for at least four decades, starting with *The Dating Game*, which first aired on ABC in 1965 and ended in 1999; on this show, a woman (on rare occasions the gender roles were switched) asks three bachelors a series of questions to help her select one for a date. Most reality dating shows prior to *The Bachelor* did not follow the development of a romantic relationship over time. The ill-fated *Who Wants to Marry a Multi-Millionaire?*, which aired on FOX in February 2000, was the first reality TV show that, like *The Bachelor* and *The Bachelorette*, explicitly identified marriage as the desired outcome for participants. On *Who Wants to Marry a Multi-Millionaire?*, a rich bachelor had the pick of fifty women from around the world who competed in various competitions (a swimsuit competition among them) and answered morality-testing questions to win his heart. When the multi-millionaire finally selected his lucky bride, they married on air. The happy outcome, however, quickly unraveled: the winner asked for an annulment right after the honeymoon.

Immediately following the successful first season of *The Bachelor*, a slew of reality romance shows emerged, including Fox's *Joe Millionaire* and NBC's *Average Joe* and *For Love or Money*, and new ones continue to pop up every season. However, only the first season of *Joe Millionaire* earned ratings to compete with *The Bachelor* and *The Bachelorette*. The debut of *Joe Millionaire* beat *The Bachelorette* debut (first season) by attracting 18.6 million viewers, 1.2 million more than the 17.4 million who tuned in for *The Bachelorette* (Robins, January 25-31, 2003, p. 53). However, the second season of *Joe Millionaire* was a ratings failure, attracting only 6.7 million viewers in the first week and dropping to 5.9 million in the second week (Paulsen, October 31, 2003), while subsequent seasons of *The Bachelor*, as discussed earlier, proved to be fairly consistent ratings successes. To date, no reality romance show on a major network has matched the success of *The Bachelor* or *The Bachelorette*. Of course, reality romance shows continue to pop up, especially on the cable networks, such as VH1's *Flavor of Love*, *I Love NY*, and *Rock of Love* (to name a few), and many are quite successful by cable standards.

Briefly, I want to note that since prime-time reality TV shows have become popular, we have witnessed a cross-pollination of some of the aesthetics of the reality TV format in scripted shows, that is, some of the formal characteristics suggesting real people doing real things are being captured on film. For instance, while the series *24* is scripted, with actors playing characters, the episodes are fashioned to look like they are in real time, the entire season representing 24 hours in the life of its characters (each one-hour episode representing an hour in the lives of the characters). Similarly, *The Office*, a half-hour scripted comedy show with actors, uses a cinema-verité documentary style of camera work to tell its story. The humor of the show relies on the discomfort surrounding the portrayal of events on the series as if these were unscripted moments performed by real people in front of a camera. The currently popular comedy *Modern Family* also uses a home-video documentary style, with handheld camera work and on-camera interviews with characters throughout the episodes. In this way, the action on the series appears as if it is a moment captured on a home video, allowing for characters to comment directly to the audience about what is happening on the series. Even the prime-time series *Grey's Anatomy*, which does not use any reality TV aesthetics, aired an episode in fall 2010, "These Arms of Mine," that was the result of a pretend documentary (in the narrative of the series a film crew came to film the doctors working) about the doctors that followed the action in the hospital over several days. What viewers watched that week was the supposed documentary produced by the fictive production company.

Racialization

Chapter 2 is devoted to a discussion of how race functions in the BI. However, I want to note from the outset that I base my noting of race on visible racial markers and comments by participants about their racial background. I am interested in how the BI constructs race—in racialization—how it treats race: who it conceives of as white, and who it conceives of as a person of color, and the consequences of these different conceptions. Some women are marked by their dark skin or physical features as women of color and are treated as such on the series. Other women who are not explicitly marked physically as women of color but are described with a specific ethnic heritage—for instance, Latin American—are marked by the series sometimes as women of color and sometimes not. Some Asian American women are marked sometimes as women of color and sometimes as white (their ethnicity erased despite visible ethnic markers). When I do not indicate a participant's race, it is because they are constructed as white within the space of the BI. This is not to endorse the assumption that whiteness is the default race (the norm), but rather because most participants in the BI are presented as white and so it becomes cumbersome to note this throughout.

Chapters

Chapter 1 sets up some of the overriding paradigms in the BI about the inter-animation of surveillance and notions of authenticity, and looks at how authenticity is aligned with whiteness. This chapter also details how the trope of confession works in the BI. Chapter 2 explores how a context can be "raced," that is, create a setting where only people constructed as a certain race (in this case, white) are privileged. This chapter also examines how, in *The Bachelor*, with twenty-five women living in the same house and at the bachelor's disposal, the Western trope of the Eastern harem structures the show, duplicating in the series the imperialist, Orientalist, and oppressive racist premises of the trope. Chapters 3 and 4 look at how women's preparedness for love is presented based on their emotional behavior. Chapter 3 argues that women in the BI need to show a specific economy in their display of emotions to remain viable romantic partners (not too much and not too little) and details how taking the necessary risk to find love is intricately related to a woman's ability to appropriately display her emotions. Chapter 3 focuses on women who are too stringent in their display of emotions. Chapter 4 examines the other extreme, the hallmark of many reality shows, the display of excessively emotional women. This chapter argues that emotional displays by women are akin to the "money shot" in film pornography. Chapter 5 situates reality TV as a rich site for the study of therapeutic culture, with its ubiquitous on-camera confessions involving talk about feelings using the language of therapy. How many times do we see someone confessing "I've learned so much about myself from this experience"? While scholars studying therapeutic culture note a constant incitement to work on, change the self, many BI participants assert a consistent, unchanged self as therapeutic. Finally, Chapter 6 explores the use of traditionally feminist paradigms of "empowerment" and "choice" in the BI. Scholars studying postfeminist discourse in popular media note the recurrent conundrum of the woman who desires it all (career, husband, and family), with the resulting tensions among work/career, love/family, and femininity/sexuality. While these desires are present in the women in the BI, the tensions seem to have disappeared. As well, the BI adds a new twist to the conventional postfeminist tension between work and love, since women in this space must first possess a career, or the possibility of a career, before they can continue on their journey to find a husband and build a family.

Notes

1.   Chapter 5 analyzes parts of Bob Guiney's book *What a Difference a Year Makes: How Life's Unexpected Setbacks Can Lead to Unexpected Joy* (2003) even though it is not part of the series, strictly speaking. Guiney's book speaks uniquely to the use of therapeutic language by participants about their experiences on the series.

2.   The format of *The Bachelor* was bought by BBC 3 in England and by TQS in Quebec.

3.   In the summer of 2010 another spin-off from *The Bachelor* aired, *Bachelor Pad*. This series is not included in the analysis or in the use of the term "BI" due to time constraints (at the time of this writing, the series just ended its run).

Chapter 1: Authenticity, Whiteness, Confession, and Surveillance

Surveillance is key in understanding the space of reality TV, since surveillance technologies are used to film people in order to gather the footage required to create the shows. One of the popular activities participants are filmed doing is confessing to the camera, forefronting their awareness of the presence of cameras and the fact of surveillance. In the space of a reality TV show, unlike in more traditional venues where surveillance has historically been used, participants are fully aware they are under surveillance. In a very literal sense, this can have a panoptic disciplining effect: aware their every move will be caught on camera and can be used in visual and auditory constructions of them in mediated products, participants regulate their behavior accordingly. This chapter lays out some of the groundwork for the complicated ways in which surveillance functions in the BI to authenticate the behaviors of participants and to privilege whiteness.

Confession

A main activity participants do on the BI, and on reality TV shows generally, is confess to a camera. Not only does reality TV offer the illusion that people are talking authentically about their thoughts and feelings (Tincknell and Raghuram, 2002, p. 205), it provides the further illusion of assurance that participants have confessed adequately—because it is, after all, caught on film. The action in the BI and the development of relationships in the BI (and in many reality TV shows) emerges through confessing and emoting on camera, particularly rele-

17

vant activities on a show that focuses on relationships and has a female target audience. These moments are crucial, as I discuss in Chapter 5, for expressions of therapeutic transformation. It is also often in these moments that participants express emotion (discussed in Chapters 3 and 4). This mirrors a trend Dovey (2000) notes of putting real people on camera expressing intimate things. "An enormous proportion of the output of factual TV is now based upon an incessant performance of identity structured through first person speaking about feelings, sentiment and, most powerfully, intimate relationships" (p. 104). In the BI, these personal ways of expressing oneself are privileged. Confession is central. The act of confession is formalistically embedded in the structure of the shows, with participants confessing to the camera in "private," or rather without any other participants present. Of course, crew members are on hand (the camera person at least).[1] These "private" moments use head shots in medium close-up and close-up (from the waist or shoulders up) and direct-address shots. The "private" on-camera moments are iconic of the reality TV genre itself, genre-specific, marked by a certain type of speech (reflections on the self, on others, and on the action on the series) and signaled through visual cues (head-shots and medium shots, people speaking directly to the camera). The settings for these vary in the BI, but the backgrounds suggest they are shot on-site. Thus, in the midst of activities, participants are given the opportunity to step away from the action and record their thoughts on-camera, in "private."[2] Often participants express their growing affection for the star, their dislike for other participants, or worries, concerns, and anxieties they have about the situation. The impression given is that we are getting a glimpse of an insider self, an "honest" self who speaks frankly to the camera about his/her feelings and thoughts, in private—without worrying others will hear (ironic considering participants have full knowledge that this footage can be aired on national television).[3] These direct-address moments are essential in constructing the narrative and, especially, in explaining participants' motives. The narrative of the series would not make sense if these scenes were removed: they are integral to the logic and to the mode of storytelling.

The series intersperses every activity with participant on-camera interviews where people confess their feelings. I turn to an example to illustrate how confession works. After the rose ceremony at the end of the first episode of season four of *The Bachelor*, slow, languid guitar music plays in the background as Heather, a twentysomething administrative assistant who has just been eliminated, walks across the carpet in the room where the rose ceremony takes place and hugs the bachelor. While this is unfolding, we hear a voice-over of Heather saying how disappointed she is, that she does not understand why this happened. We then see a close-up of her tear-stained face as she sobs and covers her face with her hands. The sobbing mounts, and we watch Heather throw her head back and drop it into her hands as she says to the camera:

> I thought Bob was so cute (sobbing). I thought he might be the one for me (sobbing). I've never really gotten my heart broken, and to get it broken on na-

tional TV is just, like, killer. Why does this have to happen to me (sobbing)?
I'm a firm believer that everything happens for a reason (sobbing), but why?

This is a "private" moment when she tells the camera her thoughts and feelings: viewers see her talking directly to the camera. The confession guides a specific narrative about what the elimination means for Heather: a sad event (she is sobbing), loss (she thought he "might be the one"), disheartening (expressing disappointment and incomprehension about why this has happened). She discloses these feelings to the camera, but this is not information she shares directly with the bachelor (Bob) or any of the other participants. The impression is that viewers are gaining access to privileged, "private" information.

Often, the series couples part of the dialogue from a "private" on-camera confession with footage from another scene: the dialogue from the private moment narrates the other scene, suggesting that the thoughts expressed during the "private" on-camera moment are ones the participant had during another scene. For instance, in the scene with Heather, we hear her talking in voice-over about how upset she is about the elimination before we see her talking directly to the camera. The voice-over narrates the scene in which she walks across the carpet to say good-bye to the bachelor and cues us to her feelings about this event, and yet, the on-camera interview had to have taken place after she leaves the rose ceremony.

The "private" on-camera confessions are actually interviews with production technicians. Participants are generally responding to questions posed by production assistants in these moments, though the series does not reference this explicitly. Based on the participants' testimonies (Guiney, 2003) and articles in the popular press about the BI shows (for instance, Graham, September 2004, p. 198-202), as well as information from John Saade and Joe Borgenicht's *Reality TV Handbook: An Insider's Guide* (2004) (Saade is a reality programming executive at ABC who developed and oversaw production of *The Bachelor*), often the on-camera "private" moments emerge in response to questions by workers on the show.

Authenticity, Naturalness, and Whiteness

A participant's perceived attitude toward surveillance in the space of reality TV is important. What is particular to reality TV is the suggestion that surveillance of the self is not only acceptable but desirable (Andrejevic, 2004, p. 145; Pecora, 2002, p. 348), inasmuch as it can be used to prove authenticity of the self (Couldry, 2002, p. 287). Paradoxically, this translates into an ability to appear under surveillance as if one is not under surveillance, mirroring how one is imagined to behave when cameras are not present. Thus, while Andrejevic (2002) suggests that part of the work of reality television is to equate surveillance of the self with comfort with oneself and self-knowledge (p. 253), part of this setup is also, implicitly, to conflate comfort with oneself with behaviors imagined to exist off-camera. In this way, not only must a participant overcome the fact of surveillance (discussed in detail shortly) to let his or her real emotions come through on-camera, but these emotions must be displayed in a manner that it is imagined the person would display them if the cameras were not rolling.

As Hardy and I (2008) outline, "Good RTV [reality TV] participants per-form not-performing" (p. 378) to achieve natural authenticity under surveillance. Participants who appear natural, authentic under surveillance, are performing in ways that are specifically deemed to be authentic or natural within the space of reality TV (King, 2005). Concomitantly, participants who are unable to perform authenticity in this way are seen as performing for the camera and therefore as inauthentic, as not belonging in that space. Authenticity and naturalness are a performance, with specific requirements. One of these requirements, I argue, is whiteness.

The BI is a space that is raced, "a space where a particular race is privi-leged" (Dubrofsky and Hardy, 2008). In this space, behaviors attached to white bodies are at an advantage, and authenticity, naturalness, and whiteness are in-tricately aligned (Dubrofsky and Hardy, 2008)—as authenticity and naturalness are most easily performed by bodies constructed as white. Participants at times express this requirement to be natural, without necessarily articulating the impli-cations or the need to do this under surveillance. For instance, on episode three of season thirteen of *The Bachelor*, Nikki tells the camera that being pretty and smart is not enough to win favor with the bachelor: a woman must also be natu-ral, something she admits is a struggle for her. Nikki is presented on the series as wanting to be in control of situations she cannot control and therefore as unable to let go and allow the natural process of finding love to unfold. She is eliminat-ed on the fourth episode. What is notable is that Nikki's problem seems to be that she cannot break the barriers preventing her from showing her natural self; her problem, effectively, is not that she is the wrong kind of person for finding love with the star but rather that she is simply unable to relax and let this authen-tic person inside her emerge (also a problem for several other participants, as I discuss below and in Chapter 3). It is this sense of revealing an identity that al-ready exists that is important in relation to whiteness. As Hardy and I contend (2008), "On *The Bachelor*, the rules of the game are to properly reveal one's authentic nature under surveillance. The identity of participants need not be spo-ken or identified; it is always already there, ready to be revealed, assumed, just like Whiteness" (p. 379). In other words, the requirements to appear natural, to appear as if one is not performing, are also the markers of whiteness, because these qualities are more easily performed by a white body in the space of white-centered reality TV shows. Conversely, authentic identity in a white-centered show is "an often difficult position for Black subjects to occupy" (Dubrofsky and Hardy, 2008, p. 377).[4] African American subjects in popular culture spaces must often actively claim an identity—this is part of the process of authentication for African American subjects—rather than "reveal" their identities, the domain of a white subject (Dubrofsky and Hardy, p. 377-379). Reality TV shows that center white participants and the need for natural authenticity to emerge thus privilege white participants, since it is white bodies that seem to most easily embody these qualities. I am not suggesting that all people of color are held to the same parameters in performing authenticity as African Americans, but rather I use this example illustratively to forefront how authenticity is raced in specific ways that privilege whiteness on white prime-time network shows.

Just as whiteness resists classification, its borders undefined (Nakayama and Krizek, 1999), so too does authenticity in the BI. Authenticity, like whiteness, is everything and nothing. It awaits to be seamlessly revealed, assumed to always already be there. If a white participant is not authentic, this is presented as the participant refusing to reveal his or her real self (hiding this real self). The test for a white participant is how well he or she is able to reveal this identity under surveillance. As suggested above, this presents a problem for African American participants, for instance, since actively claiming an identity (often the only way for African American participants to establish an identity in the space of reality TV) inevitably reveals them as performing for the camera and therefore as not-natural, as inauthentic in the space of white-centered reality TV shows.

However, as discussed in Chapter 2, women of color in the BI rarely have to show or prove their authenticity. They are deemed neither authentic nor inauthentic. Authenticity is not a quality relevant to their tenure on the show because they are not part of the central action of the series: finding love. Women of color are not even part of the story about women failing at love.

Authenticity, Surveillance, and Contrived Contexts

The potential awkwardness of being under surveillance, of doing what might normally be thought of as private activities on camera, works in some ways to verify the authenticity of what participants are experiencing and the emotions they display. The contrived context of a reality TV show (the setting, lighting, organized activities, presence of TV workers, and so forth) works in a similar fashion. In the space of the BI, a participant's ability to confess emotions under surveillance, and in the contrived setting of the reality TV show, confirms the realness and authenticity of the emotions: so strong were the feelings that they emerged despite the surveilled and produced context. As Jones (2003) explains in her discussion of *Big Brother* UK,

> Ironically it is the very constructedness of the *Big Brother* game show that appears to liberate the content. Its artifice is so transparent, the message to the

viewer is that, yes, the cameras are present, no pretence, we can all see them, now let's get on with capturing actuality. Whereas audiences often question the fidelity of truth claims in factual programs, *Big Brother* audiences appeared to be able to suspend their disbelief and look for the reality created within the artifice. (p. 418)

In fact, the relationship between authenticity and artifice is more codependent than Jones articulates and is crucially linked to the irony of the series. The artifice allows for the construction of authenticity rather than, as Jones suggests, the artifice being bypassed, a step on the way to capturing authenticity. It is upon the apparent artifice of the show, and indeed the seeming irony, that the apparent authenticity of the action rests. While scripted programs often aim to show "realistic" and authentic characters and to approximate real emotions and situations, reality shows make the actual construction of authenticity central; this is the very basis for the action of the show. As Murray and Ouellette (2009) note, reality TV fuses "popular entertainment with a self-conscious claim to the discourse of the real" (p. 3), suggesting that such shows' "fixation with 'authentic' personalities, situations, and narratives is considered to be reality TV's primary distinction from fictional television and also its primary selling point" (p. 5). Reality TV, with its suggestion of showing real people doing real things, foregrounds how notions of real, authentic, surveilled selves are constructed, at the same time that it denies this construction by claiming to have access to the real. As well, as Murray and Ouellette (2009) also observe, while reality TV "whets our desire for the authentic, much of our engagement with such texts paradoxically hinges on our awareness that what we are watching is constructed and contains 'fictional' elements" (p. 7). It is this interplay between explicitly contrived and surveilled contexts and access to the real that produces authenticity: being able to show emotion in this context verifies a participant as authentic, and awareness on the part of the participant that the situation is contrived makes the emotions displayed that much more authentic.

I return to the Heather example to discuss how surveillance functions in authenticating participants, especially their displays of emotion. Several things are striking about the moment above with Heather: the display of such intense emotion after spending but one evening with the bachelor (and twenty-four other women); the fact that Heather barely figures in the episode until this moment at the very end; and her discomfort with having her heart broken on national TV. Heather's uncontrollable sobbing defines her presence. This incident is but one from what is likely hours of footage of Heather doing all manner of things, but this is the one selected of her. This scene highlights the requirement for the women to show a certain economy of emotion: not too much, and not too little (discussed in Chapters 2 and 3). Heather clearly shows too much emotion and embodies the kind of woman who will not find love on the series. And she is doubly damned because she did this despite the surveillance aspect of the series, thus confirming her emotions (these were so strong that even the fact of surveillance cannot stop her from expressing them). Indeed, a notable aspect of this scene is Heather's acute awareness of her predicament: "and to get my heart broken on national TV is just, like, killer."

In some ways, the scene with Heather can be read as potentially ironic. Her awareness of feeling such emotion on television and the excessiveness of her emotions almost read as comical (seeing as she just met the bachelor), suggesting perhaps that viewers are meant to see in this scene the potential absurdity of the setup of the series. These types of scenes (common in the BI) speak to Cloud's (2010)[5] argument that *The Bachelor* "invites two kinds of investment simultaneously: the pleasure of the romantic fantasy and the pleasure of irony in recognizing the fantasy's folly" (p. 414). Authenticity is actually produced through the interplay of irony, potential recognition of the unrealizability of the romantic fantasy, surveillance, and the constructedness of the situation. As Johnston (2006) notes, despite the artifice of *The Bachelor*, what is important to viewers is that moments of emotional truth emerge (p. 118). Part of how this occurs is due to the surveilled and contrived context and the participant's awareness of this context (and of the potential outlandishness of trying to find love in this manner): despite these things, real emotions are felt by participants and shown to viewers. In this way then, Heather's exclamation about the misfortune of this all happening on TV serves to show that what we are witnessing is authentic—her feelings are so real that not even her knowledge of surveillance (of being recorded for television) can prevent her from expressing herself. This suggests that what we just saw should be understood as being very real, paradoxically, not only despite its being recorded for national TV, despite Heather's awareness of the situation, but ultimately because of this. No matter the situation, surveillance, and Heather's self-awareness, we are to read Heather's emotions as very real, even if the context in which they arise may seem rather unbelievable.

The interanimation of constructedness and authenticity in the context of surveillance is also exemplified in the "After the Final Rose" episode of the second season of *The Bachelorette*. On one side of a split screen is the host, Chris Harrison, on the other is Keisha, a young African American woman holding a microphone in Times Square in New York City. She asks Ian McKee, the bachelorette's chosen man from season two who is with Chris, what made him change his mind and ultimately propose? Cut to a medium shot of Ian sitting on a couch on a stage (in front of a live studio audience) next to Meredith Phillips (the starring bachelorette). He says:

> I think that my love was there the whole time and my biggest concern was whether or not I was going to propose there in front of the rest of the world. It just didn't seem like me, and when I finally got before her, all the walls that I'd built, these rules that I'd made for myself, came tumbling down and the emotion just took me over and I became powerless.

Ian acknowledges both the contrived nature of the situation (the reservations he had about proposing "in front of the rest of the world") and the feelings of love and emotion that overtook him during the series. Andrejevic (2004) suggests that reality TV shows accurately portray the "reality of contrivance" (p. 17), and paradoxically, it is often the very obviousness of the contrived nature of the show that foregrounds the authenticity of some of the action. Thus, Ian tells us that his feelings were there all along and were so strong that ultimately the constructed nature of the series seemed irrelevant in the face of such real, genuine, and strong emotions: he had to be true to his feelings and do what he would have done if the cameras had not been present. The power of love is affirmed as it is able to break down Ian's walls, or as he puts it his "rules" about how one should behave under surveillance. What is expressed is the strength and realness of his feelings (there all along waiting to come out), not the difficulty of feeling real emotions in such a contrived scenario. In fact, according to the logic of the space of reality TV, an inability to show one's feelings under surveillance proves that the feelings are not genuine enough (if they were, they would burst forth despite the context).

Another illustrative example emerges during the episode when Matthew, the second runner-up for Meredith's heart, requests time with Meredith in private (that is, without Ian present). He tells Meredith he feels she led him on. Meredith responds by admitting she lied on the series and explains that she did so out of insecurity and because of the stressful nature of the situation. While many on the show have often commented (while on the series and afterward) about the stressful nature of the series, few admit to lying. But Meredith's lying becomes inconsequential in the grand scheme of things. At one point Meredith tells Matthew that on her final date with him she felt she was playing a game and that this was distressing since she did not want to play games. The liveness of the show (it aired live; usually these episodes are taped in front of a studio audience), combined with the seemingly forthright admission by Meredith about her discomfort with the constructed and contrived nature of the series, reinforces the fact that what is presented is the real result of a difficult process. The outcome is real: Ian and Meredith find true love (the show suggests); Matthew is a genuinely sweet man who was hurt in the process. Confirmed is the sense that the people on the series are real and behave out of genuine emotion, and in so doing are able to overcome the difficulties of the constructed nature of the series.

As well, in the second episode of the three-part special "Trista and Ryan's Wedding" (which shows the preparations for Trista and Ryan's wedding, the bachelor and bachelorette parties, and the wedding), Ryan gets angry at the makers of the show for setting up a bachelor party where he is encouraged to do things he does not want to do and feels would upset Trista (be intimate with other women). In a drunken rage, he leaves the scene of the party, rips off his microphone and goes AWOL for several hours. When Trista finds out he is missing, she is frantic with worry. Finally, she runs off to find privacy, begging the crew to leave her alone. She locks herself in the bathroom, and while we cannot see her, we hear her sobbing (her mic was still attached).

The climactic moment comes at the end, when Trista and Ryan are reunited. They embrace for a very long time, Trista in tears and Ryan near tears, and they profess their love for one another and their desire to never be apart again. The episode's narrative actually sets up the constructedness of the situation as the central problem the couple in love must overcome to find each other. Ultimately, Trista and Ryan's love is so strong, and they trust each other so much, that the contrived setup of the special cannot stand in the way of their being together: the harrowing experience of the bachelor party and the meddling of producers works to strengthen and reaffirm the couple's devotion to one another.

Increasingly, as seasons progress, realness seeps into the BI in the form of the lives of participants outside the context of the series. This occurs especially in the last seasons of *The Bachelor* and *The Bachelorette*. Prior to this, the lives of participants outside the show rarely became a significant part of the action on the series or had a significant impact on the outcome of a season. The effect is to make viewers aware that the series is a contrived setting, a time-out from the actual real lives of participants, while at the same time confirming that what occurs on the series is real, has real consequences for the lives of participants. On season fourteen of *The Bachelor*, for instance, Ali has an emotional breakdown when her work calls and tells her to choose between staying on the show and returning to her job (so she can keep her job). She leaves the show. This event becomes a major segment of that episode and part of the storyline on a later episode when she asks the star, Jake, if she can return because she realizes she made the wrong choice (he refuses). Similarly, on season five of *The Bachelorette*, Ed Swiderski is faced with the same choice, work or the show. He also leaves, choosing work. This difficult decision becomes a focal point of that episode. However, when he asks to return shortly after, Jillian Harris welcomes him back (ultimately choosing him as her final man). Season six of *The Bachelorette* is particularly plagued by interference from the outside lives of participants. Several episodes in, it is discovered that Justin, one of the participants vying for Ali's affections, has several girlfriends back home. He exits dramatically and Ali is furious. As well, Frank, one of the final three men Ali chooses, comes to the realization that he is still in love with his ex-girlfriend right before his overnight date with Ali. The series shows his reunion with this woman and his subsequent breakup with Ali, as well as Ali's heartbreak.

Like Ian above, Jason, star of season thirteen of *The Bachelor*, explains to Chris in the "After the Final Rose Part II" episode that he cared so much about Molly (the second runner-up) that he went through the ordeal of publicly breaking up with Melissa Rycroft (the woman he chose on the finale) on the "After the Final Rose Part I." He explains to Chris in part II of this episode that his actions express his love for Molly, telling Chris that he stands by his decision and that in the end all the obstacles he faced were worth it. When the couple appears on "The Women Tell All" for season five of *The Bachelorette* to give an update on their relationship, Chris states that everything they went through was either going to bring them together or rip them apart. Molly responds by affirming that being together is what allowed them to make it through these difficult times. Here the obstacles the series presents are valiantly overcome in the name of love, and overcoming these serves as a testament to the feelings of the participants as well as proof of the sacrifices they were willing to make to be together.

In perhaps one of the more unusual twists in the BI, and one that especially calls attention to the contrived context in which the action of the series takes place, a storyline appears on season fourteen of *The Bachelor* about one of the participants, Roslyn, having an inappropriate relationship with a producer on the show. Details about the inappropriateness of the relationship are never provided, but Roslyn is asked to leave and the producer is fired. Though Roslyn is asked to leave early on, the situation is discussed in detail much later on the "Women Tell All" episode, where Roslyn is brought on stage for a rather explosive exchange with Chris. On this episode, Jake (the star) and Chris comment on how this situation caught them by surprise and Chris notes that he was having to improvise in handling the situation since this was a first. Jake calls the moment a kind of reality check, telling the audience that the incident made him question why he was there and wonder if he'd made the right decision to be on the show. He says that in the end, the incident helped him clarify that he was there to find the girl he is going to marry. In this way, an unpredictable obstacle, this time in part from within the show (the actions of a producer), works to highlight that the makers of the series (including the host) can be surprised by what transpires on the series, that it is an unpredictable context, that anything can happen. And ultimately the context helps Jake reaffirm his commitment to finding love.

Including these unpredictable moments works in two strategic ways. For one, it highlights that the participants are real people with ongoing lives that are impacted by what happens on the series and emphasizes that what occurs on the series is a meaningful part of their lives, with important implications. Secondly, the more the tropes of the series become familiar to viewers as seasons progress, the more that moments where the lives of participants outside the series interfere with the narrative of the BI, or where participants (such as Rosyln) exceed the confines of the series, become important in confirming for audiences that there is always an element of the unpredictable despite the predictability and contrived nature of the series; because, after all, we are dealing with real people with real lives.

Notes

1.   Participants in these instances speak to the camera in different settings, and the camera does not remain static and immobile as it does when not manned by a person.

2.   These are not moments shot in a location designated for "private," on-camera confessions, as is the case in some reality shows such as *Real World* and *Big Brother*,

where viewers know as soon as they see a participant in that particular setting (generally the same one throughout the series) that the participant is confessing in "private" to the camera.

3. Item 10 of the eligibility requirements listed on *The Bachelor* website (http://thebachelor.warnerbros.com/web/eligibility.jsp) stipulates that participants understand and agree "that he or she . . . may be audio and/or video taped twenty-four (24) hours a day, seven (7) days a week while participating in the Program by means of open and hidden cameras, whether or not he or she is then aware that he or she is being video-taped or recorded . . . and that such Recordings may be disseminated on television and/or all media now known or hereafter devised, in any and all manner throughout the Universe in perpetuity."

4. For a more detailed discussion of authenticity as it is aligned with whiteness and the complicated relationship between black bodies and authenticity in popular media texts, please see Dubrofsky and Hardy (2008).

5. Cloud's article was published just as I was completing final edits on this book. In addition to her thoughts about irony, Cloud touches briefly on many issues covered in this book, including the use of sincerity and authenticity, the emptiness of the promises of love, the sexist competition, the punishment of women who are seen as insincere in their quest for love, and the exhortation to express and confess feelings. Unfortunately, I was not able to fully address Cloud's arguments at this late date.

Chapter 2: Whiteness in the Harem

When an early version of this chapter appeared in article form in the journal *Critical Studies in Media Communication* (CSMC) in 2006, there was no work on the topic of race and reality TV, barring a handful of articles. However, reality TV is a television genre where people of color are featured, and a rich body of critical scholarship on the topic is emerging (examples include Andrejevic and Colby, 2006; Boylorn, 2008; Harvey, 2006; Hasinoff, 2008). In addition, a special issue of CSMC, edited by Orbe (2008), has been devoted to the topic. My contribution to this ongoing conversation turns attention to the romance genre and to how people of color figure in a white-centered show. This chapter updates the earlier article, which ended with season eight. Incorporating seasons nine through fourteen opens up additional questions about postracist discourse, the use of racially ambiguous women, patriotism, the use of exotic locales in recentering whiteness, and the representation of Asian American women.

This chapter argues that the BI is raced, creating a habitus where whiteness is privileged (a white space, a context in which only "white" people can fall in love), and promotes a version of love that works only for white people. The space is an oppressive and racist context in which women of color can never figure as viable romantic partners but rather work to facilitate the process of two white people finding love. The chapter looks at women of color, examining how they somehow never "matter" when it comes to the central action of the BI. In this way, women of color are not centered in any of the important tropes on which the action of the series relies: authenticity (discussed in Chapter 1); emotional displays (explored in Chapter 3 and Chapter 4); therapeutic transformation (the focus of Chapter 5); and notions of choice and empowerment (examined in Chapter 6). I focus primarily on *The Bachelor* because women of color figure only in this series (there are no starring women of color in *The Bachelorette*).[1]

As mentioned in the introduction, I base my noting of race on visible racial markers and comments by participants about their racial background. I examine racialization, which means looking at the social construction of race. I do not rely on an essential notion of race. However, marking race is complicated when dealing with a visual medium. As Hyun Yi Kang (2002) argues, to trouble understandings of racial categories, we must be mindful to avoid reducing race to bodies. Nonetheless, in this medium, "what *matters* . . . is the illusion of human *bodies*" (Hyun Yi Kang, p. 99). Some women are marked as women of color by their dark skin or physical features and are treated as such on the series. Some women are not specifically marked as women of color through their appearance; however, they are described as having a particular ethnic heritage. For example, women of Latin descent have fluid racial identities, sometimes constructed as women of color, sometimes not. The same thing happens with Asian women, who while often possessing physical markers that suggest they are Asian are nonetheless treated as white—or rather, as an ideal version of white, a model minority. However, Asian women are also at times treated as women of color.

The BI uses the rhetoric of realism (through its form and content: the activities of real people doing real things, two people finding real love) and naturalizes the constructions of race it promotes. The BI exhibits strategic whiteness: recenters whiteness, maintains whiteness as the norm and makes whiteness implicitly the desirable and, in fact, the only option. Strategic whiteness is apparent structurally, visually, and narratively, and works to continue a neocolonialist project that represents people of color as "different from and therefore inferior to the dominant political group in order to ensure its power" (Projansky and Ono, 1999, p. 152). This neocolonial context situates marginalized characters, often people of color, in the service of a "pedagogy" in which certain racial and other hierarchies are affirmed and maintained (Ono, 2000).

By focusing on the nonprimary participants, the marginalized characters, I am insisting on the importance of looking at people of color in programs where they are not foregrounded (the norm in many popular television shows). This addresses the ways in which shows structure the status of people of color as secondary and how minor characters work through a larger power structure that foregrounds whiteness (Ono, 2000, p. 180). Nakayama and Krizek (1999) contend that whiteness gains much of its power by resisting "any extensive characterization that would allow for the mapping of its contours" (p. 88). I explicitly map out the contours of whiteness in the BI. I ask: how is it that while there are a range of ways in which the BI shows white women behaving that allow them to participate in the central romance narrative of the series, almost none of the narrower range of ways women of color behave include active participation in the romance narrative? How does the harem structure of the series situate race and experiences with racial "others" as both a necessary part of the journey of finding love for white people and as something that must be overcome? This chapter examines some of this "commonsense" rhetoric to unpack how the BI naturalizes the process of a white man and woman as the culminating pair.

A Nod and a Wave Good-bye to Women of Color

While women of color appear on the show, they do not thrive. In the first season of *The Bachelor*, all four women of color in the initial pool are eliminated by the third week. In the second season, the last two of the three women of color voluntarily leave during the second week. The only woman of color on the third season is eliminated the first week. All three women of color on the fourth season are eliminated by the sixth week. On the fifth season, all four women of color are eliminated by the second week. On the sixth season, the last of the three women of color in the original pool is eliminated by the fourth week. However, a Cuban American woman, Mary, joins the series on the third episode of the sixth season, and she is the woman bachelor Byron finally chooses as his mate. This is the first time the series adds women in the middle of a season (a white woman is added along with Mary). Mary also appeared in season four, when the series marks her explicitly as Cuban American. In season six, her ethnicity is not mentioned until the second-to-last episode. I argue below that while Mary is marked as a woman of color in season four, she is effectively "whitened" in season six. Because she is not marked physically as a woman of color, the series can represent her ethnicity in a mutable fashion. The only woman of color on the seventh season is eliminated at the first rose ceremony. The three women of color on the eighth season are eliminated on the first episode. There are no women of color on the ninth season. On the tenth season, three of the four women of color are eliminated by the fifth episode. Tessa Horst, the final woman chosen by Andy Baldwin on season ten, is mixed race Asian American, but just as with Mary in season six, her ethnicity is never mentioned (discussed below). On season eleven, all three women of color are eliminated by the fourth week. On season twelve, the only woman of color is eliminated in week five. On season thirteen, none of the women are marked explicitly as women of color, though some of the women are racially ambiguous. For instance, Nicole (last name is "Mah") is probably mixed race Asian, though visually she is not explicitly marked as such. She is eliminated on the first episode. As well, Racquel, white in her physical appearance, is identified as Brazilian and speaks with a Brazilian accent. In addition, her characterization centers on her "foreignness" and her love of dancing (dancing is often used as a marker of Latin ethnicity in popular culture). Racquel is eliminated on the second episode. Finally, Naomi is not marked racially, but in her physical appearance she could be Latina or mixed-race (black and white). As well, her father is named Hector, a typical Latino name, suggesting she is Latina. Naomi is eliminated on episode six.[2] On season fourteen, there is only one woman of color, Channy, who is Cambodian. She is eliminated on the first episode. All the stars of *The Bachelor* and *The Bachelorette* have been white.[3]

As the above indicates, most seasons of *The Bachelor* included at least two to four women explicitly marked as women of color. However, in recent seasons (thirteen and fourteen in particular), the series has featured a mostly white cast, with season thirteen featuring a few women who are racially ambiguous, that is, women who can be read as a number of different races and who are depicted without any overarching racialization. As Valdivia (2005) argues, using racially ambiguous characters is economically advantageous in popular media texts because of the potential for characters to be read as standing in for a wide range of racial identities, allowing audiences multiple positions of racialized identification. Moreover, racially ambiguous characters are incredibly efficient in terms of meeting the requirement for representation, since one body can represent a multiplicity of racialized bodies (Valdivia, 2005). In this way, the BI can do away with women of color and instead include a racially ambiguous woman who can signify several women of color. Ono (2008) suggests that the racially ambiguous character is troubling, since he or she provides an identity at the service of other racialized identities and is ultimately identity-less, signifying only inasmuch as he or she can gesture toward an identity this person is seen as not possessing entirely (Ono, 2008, p. 138). This type of identity works as a kind of blank slate upon which other identities can be inscribed.

This trend toward fewer racially marked women in the BI perhaps signals a movement from an assimilationist to a postracial cultural context. As Esposito (2009) articulates, "the term 'postracial' has been utilized in increasing amounts in the media to denote some people's perceptions that the election of Barack Obama marks a new era in our society—one in which race no longer matters" (p. 52). The disappearance of women of color from *The Bachelor* suggests it is no longer necessary to gesture toward multicultural and inclusionary practices: we have moved beyond the need for such things because racism is no longer an issue. In this way, an all-white cast poses no problem, since the final selection of women is a result of a natural selection process not of racist practices. As well, a racially ambiguous character gestures toward inclusionary practices while at the same time foreclosing any actual engagement with issues of difference.

Focusing on women of color is tricky. Because they figure so little in the BI, one risks seeming to be making "too much" of "too little." Though nearly all participants marked as women of color on *The Bachelor* are eventually eliminated, perhaps it is statistically insignificant that only two women of color (neither marked as women of color) ended up with a bachelor at the end of the season. Perhaps most of the women of color never "clicked" romantically with the bachelors.

Inferential Racism: Centering Whiteness

The BI invites viewers to consider race within the logic of relational choice rather than within the logic of representation. What is crucial is how consistently the series marks the presence of the women of color. Appadurai (1996) suggests that universities often encourage diversity on "the principle that more difference is better" but frequently fail to create "a habitus where diversity is at the heart of the apparatus itself" (p. 26). This is also true of television. The BI habitus is such that women of color exist but are mostly irrelevant to the dominant narrative, except to the extent that their actions work to frame the white women's access to this narrative or to frame the white star's journey to finding his ideal mate. In other words, the racism is not overt. At times it is difficult to pin down. This is what Hall (2003) calls "inferential racism": when racist representations are unspoken and naturalized, making the racist premises upon which the representations rely difficult to bring to the surface (p. 91).

Women of color on the BI verify the behavior of white women and thus recenter whiteness, generally framing the white women's illegitimate behavior (their excessive emotional behavior) and highlighting that these particular women are unsuitable matches for the bachelor. Women of color function as window dressing for the white women, giving them a "special flavor, an added spice" (hooks, 1992, p. 157)—in this case not one that makes the white women more romantically attractive. However, the women of color are not, in and of themselves, legitimate contestants for love.

For example, Anindita, a South Asian American woman who leaves at the second rose ceremony on the second season, causes quite a stir during a group date with bachelor Aaron Buerge and four white women. One of the women on the date, Christi (discussed in Chapter 4), expresses her dislike for one of the other women on the date, Suzanne. Anindita confronts Christi about her behavior toward Suzanne. The central focus of the scene, however, is on how hurt Christi is by the day's events. In fact, during the confrontation, Anindita's voice is heard but she appears only in the corner of the frame. What is apparent is Christi's emotion, with close-ups of her teary face. While Anindita exposes the tension between the two women—she is shown to incite it—she is never central to this narrative, much less to the romance narrative with the bachelor. Anindita's function is to highlight Christi's excessive emotionality.

Karin, an African American woman, acts to frame and recenter the presence of a white woman, Lee-Ann (discussed in detail in Chapter 4), in the fourth season. Although Karin makes it to the fourth rose ceremony, she is never seen interacting with the bachelor. That she remains on the show for so long perhaps indicates some contact with Bob Guiney, yet the focus is on Bob's interactions with the other women, never with her. In fact, the series refers to her in only three ways: as beautiful (by Bob and the other women); as high-maintenance (by the other women); and as a great friend (by Lee-Ann).

Karin has little or no screen time. Although the other women refer to Karin as high-maintenance and comment on her lack of enthusiasm for the day's group date at a water park, this receives little attention. Nor does her friendship with Lee-Ann, a much disliked fellow-participant, emerge as an issue. The absence of any fuss over Karin's marked lack of enthusiasm or her closeness to a detested participant is curious, considering that whenever any of the white women set themselves apart from the main action of the series (by being disdainful of activities, aloof, self-absorbed, and so forth), this becomes a focus of at least one episode and thereafter marks the woman negatively. In essence, although the series presents Karin behaving like some of the white women, she does not signify in the same ways.

Karin's most notable moment is when she tries to comfort Lee-Ann, who is furious with the other women and with the bachelor. At this point, Karin speaks for longer (and not very long at that) than she has at any other time. Lee-Ann has been the dramatic center of much of the last four episodes (because she sets herself apart from the other women and incurs their disdain). Karin's interactions with Lee-Ann foreground this drama. To some extent, as Wallace (1990) and Projansky (2001) note about media treatment of African Americans, Karin is very visible but has no voice. Comments about Karin repeatedly reference her beauty, yet she herself rarely speaks and little attention is paid to her behavior.

Frances, an Asian American woman on the second season, figures only nominally on the show, but she centers the overemotional behavior of a white woman, Heather (not the Heather discussed in the previous chapter). The series does not show Frances interacting with the bachelor on her only date with him (a group date), although she does narrate a lot of the action on the date. However, in "The Women Tell All" episode, Frances becomes the catalyst for an emotional outburst from Heather. Frances jokes about how Heather cooked lots of good food for the women in an attempt to fatten them up. While all the women laugh, the next shot shows Heather bursting into tears. When the host asks what is wrong, Heather claims Frances's comment hurt her. Frances looks confused but apologizes. Frances's fleeting presence serves to characterize a white woman as excessively emotional.

Marshana, the only African American woman on season twelve, remains until episode five, no small feat for an African American woman on this series. Marshana fulfils many of the conventional roles played by women of color in the BI. On the first episode, Marshana complains about Stacy, a white woman, saying she's a "bitch," "loud," "belligerent," "tacky," "classless," and "riding my nerves like a pony," thus highlighting and framing the inappropriate behavior of a white woman. Stacy takes up a lot of space on this episode. She is shown behaving outrageously, drinking excessively, removing her thong and stuffing it into the bachelor's pocket. Shots of the bachelor looking very uncomfortable because of Stacy's behavior are frequent. Of course, Stacy is eliminated at the end of the first episode.

The pattern of women of color framing the behavior of white women continues throughout the series. If the explicit aim of the series is to promote romance and winners are those who succeed in becoming the star of the romance narrative (often because, in a spectacular manner, they fail to win the bachelor's affections), then the overriding message is that women of color do not count. They are positioned as neither legitimate nor illegitimate romantic partners for the bachelor. Yet, the women of color are a vital part of the story of two white people finding a partner: they verify the bachelor's choices by highlighting the unsuitability of certain white women, and they serve as window dressing for the white women (hooks, 1992, p. 157).

Assimilationist Paradigm and Choice

Despite the show's avowed attempt to offer *all* the women the opportunity for love with the bachelor and the power to make choices, these are seriously circumscribed when it comes to women of color. Gray (1995) explains that what he calls assimilationist programs "celebrate racial invisibility and color blindness . . . [by integrating] individual black characters into hegemonic white worlds void of any hint of African American traditions, social struggle, racial conflicts, and cultural difference" (p. 85). In contrast to the hegemonic status of whiteness in these texts, Gray adds, "Blackness simply works to reaffirm, shore up, and police the cultural and moral boundaries of the existing racial order. From the privileged angle of their normative race and class positions, whites are portrayed as sympathetic advocates for the elimination of prejudice" (p. 87). The overriding assimilationist paradigm of the BI is apparent in the setup of the series: by pairing white men with women of color (and white women with the few men of color on *The Bachelorette*), the series constructs these men and women as implicitly willing to engage in interracial relationships. On the surface, the series operates as if color does not matter, as if people in the series (and implicitly the makers of the show) are neutral when it comes to racial differences, or cultural differences read as racial ones, and will treat everyone as if these differences do not exist. Everyone, ostensibly, can compete to win the rewards of the show—finding a romantic partner. The suggestion is that white women and women of color have access to the same choices, will benefit from the same rewards, and will suffer the same consequences for the choices they make. However, the choices and opportunities afforded women of color do not allow access to the central romance narrative, as they do for white women. The actions of women of color do not bring them closer to winning the bachelor's heart, though it is often their job to highlight what the white women do that makes them undesirable to the bachelor.

The rose ceremony on the second episode of season two, for example, illustrates how the choices of women of color are framed. The host explains to the fifteen remaining women that the bachelor has to eliminate five of them at this rose ceremony. He reminds them, as he has before, that they have control in this situation, that they can turn down a rose if they are not interested in the bachelor. Shortly thereafter, the host reenters the room with bachelor Aaron. Aaron takes his place at the end of the room, next to the podium with the roses. As he is about to begin selecting women to remain on the show, Anindita (the South Asian American woman mentioned earlier) interrupts him, walks toward him, and tells him she feels that, to be fair to the process of the show, she should leave. She reassures him that she thinks he is a good guy but that she does not want a rose from him. They hug, and Anindita walks out of the room. Then Frances (the Asian American woman mentioned earlier) tells Aaron she also feels it is time for her to go (no reason given). She and Aaron hug, and she walks out of the room to murmurs and gasps of surprise from the other women. One unidentifiable female voice exclaims in the background that this is not right, which has the effect of emphasizing that this is not only an unusual turn of events but also that the women's actions run counter to the expectations of how the women are supposed to behave. Chris then appears next to Aaron and says that while everyone is a little surprised by this turn of events, "we respect their choice." Aaron begins the rose ceremony, saying "Well, this only goes to show that I made the right choices."

What is striking about this incident is that the only women who voluntarily leave this rose ceremony are also, apparently, the only two women of color. Though women do leave voluntarily at rose ceremonies in other seasons, it is nonetheless rare, and this is the only time two women leave at once. The assimilationist paradigm of the series constructs Frances and Anindita's decision to leave as being about choice, a choice afforded all the women, even though the hegemony and pressure of the show advocates for the choice of staying. The series illustrates Probyn's (1993) notion of "choiceoisie" (explored in detail in Chapter 6), in which women making socially validated choices are represented as making choices independently based on individual motives (of their own volition, without social or economic pressure). In this case, the socially validated choice is influenced by the racist harem structure of the series. This representation of choice fits with what Cloud (1996) calls "the rhetoric of tokenism": a liberal notion of an autonomous individual, an individual free of oppression who is able to succeed should he or she have the necessary drive to do so (see also Lubiano, 1997, p. viii). Oppression becomes personal suffering, and success is the result of individual accomplishment (Cloud, 1996, p. 119). In this context, the series shows Anindita's and Frances's decisions to leave as the result of personal choice and as having nothing to do with how the structure of the series positions women of color. They choose to leave the series; therefore they choose not to succeed at romance on the show. The words of the host immediately before the women leave (telling them that they can always exercise their right to leave) and after they leave ("we respect their choice") reinforce the idea that this is a choice the women decide to make not an action resulting from overriding structural determinants related to the show.

Perhaps Aaron's statement after Frances's and Anindita's departure is the most telling: "Well, this only goes to show that I made the right choices." In other words, Aaron is not romantically interested in the two women. Their presence, departure, or feelings for him are irrelevant as are, ultimately, their choices. In the few other instances of women departing from the series, the bachelor either makes no comment or expresses regret that a woman left.

Inferential Ethnic Presences: The Harem

Shohat (1991) suggests that one way to look at texts is to explore their *"inferential ethnic presences*, that is, the various ways in which ethnic cultures penetrate the screen without always literally being represented by ethnic and racial themes or even characters" (p. 223). The inferential ethnic presence of the harem trope in the BI reminds us, as Ono (2009) insists is the problem with neocolonialism, that part of the difficulty of discussing colonialism today is its "ghost-like presence... [that it is] not commonly recognized as part of contemporary [U.S.] culture" (p. 4). While the premise of the series, to find the bachelor a long-term romantic partner, may not immediately bring to mind the concept of the harem, the very setup of *The Bachelor* implicitly references the harem: one man with twenty-five beautiful women who live in the same quarters and are always at the bachelor's disposal. In fact, the women have little to do but lounge around and wait to share time with the bachelor. The harem trope is a Western version of the East, Hollywood's interpretation of the Eastern harem. It exists only in the Western mind (Said, 1978; Ahmed, 1982). As Said's (1978) influential work on Orientalism suggests, the Western view of the "Orient" is primarily a discourse that reinscribes and bolsters the West's view of itself; it is much less about the "Orient" than about the West. Thus, the harem becomes a place where white, Western men can dominate Eastern women. The powerful, masculine West dominates the weaker, feminized East. Shohat and Stam (1994) write:

> The popular image-making of the orient internalized the codes of male-oriented travel narratives. Strong continuities link Hollywood's ethnography with Hollywood's pornography, which often latently inscribes harems and despots even in texts not set in the orient. What might be called "harem structures" in fact permeated Western mass-mediated culture. Busby Berkeley's production numbers, for example, project a harem-like structure reminiscent of Hollywood's mythical orient; like the oriental harem, they house a multitude of women serving, as Lucy Fischer suggests, as signifiers of male power over infinitely substitutable females. The *mise-en-scène* of both harem scenes and musical numbers is structured around the scopic privilege of the master in an exclusionary space inaccessible to other men. (p. 164)

The women on *The Bachelor* are often so similar in appearance (e.g., body size and skin color) that, at least visually, they at times appear to be interchangeable. The show's structure is such that the supply of willing women—willing to make themselves accessible to this one man, and no other man, for the duration of the show—is endless. The series adds to the harem structure the notion of choice (discussed in Chapter 6): the women's willingness is bolstered by the paradigm of choice, since the women are told (each week on earlier seasons) that they can choose to leave, or to stay and accept the will of the bachelor (who will decide if they stay or leave).

The mise-en-scène in the series visually reinforces the harem structure. In describing postcards of women in harems at the turn of the century, Alloula (1986) mentions the need for a certain visual setting to effectively signify the qualities of the harem:

> The photographer carefully orchestrates his effects, so to speak, and the idea of the harem as a labyrinthine space underscores the importance of the backdrop, which consists entirely of a succession of secret alcoves, hidden doors, court-yards leading to more courtyards and so on. (p. 72)

The décor of the bachelor pad mimics this construction of the harem, with its sumptuous, boudoir-like furniture, its array of sitting rooms with stuffed couches, throw rugs, and oversized pillows and its wall hangings in rich dark colors. Of course, the requisite hot tub and swimming pool are nestled in a lush garden, with many verdant private settings for midnight trysts. The harem décor persists throughout the show. Almost every date is located near a pool and a hot tub (or this is the final destination of the date), and the many private rooms (with candles, carpets, pillows, and a fireplace) are conducive to intimacy. Settings for most dates have a harem-like décor. For instance, in episode four of season thirteen of *The Bachelor*, the women are on a group date with Jason in a hotel suite (often the location for dates), with each room decked out (as they usually are on the series) with overstuffed cushions, deep-colored plush curtains, candles, lots of flowers (bringing the harem courtyard garden indoors), and many places for lounging.

The harem theme persists in the activities on dates, where the bachelor sometimes has the opportunity to share intimacies with several women in a single night. For example, on a group date he may spend time with all the women together and then divide his time between kissing one woman in a secluded garden area, "making-out" with another in an intimate boudoir-like room, and embracing yet a third in a hot tub. The sexually charged atmosphere is enhanced by the "far-Eastern," "Orientalist" themes of the activities as well as the settings, many requiring participants to stay low to the ground, ever ready for a "tumble in the hay." In season one, for example, bachelor Alex Michel and Amanda Marsh (his final chosen woman) enjoy sushi in a private room with vaguely "Oriental" red tapestries on the wall; they sit at a low table with a carved-out floor for their feet (it looks like they are sitting on the floor). After dinner, they roll over onto the floor and "make-out." Then they move into another private room, don kimonos, and give each other full-body massages. In season four, bachelor Bob and three of the women go to a karaoke pajama party. Wearing negligee-like attire, the women sing to Bob and lounge together on deep plush red cushions. Bob "makes-out" with one of the women in the more private, curtained-off rooms in the back, adorned with a bed and pillows in deep shades of red and an "Oriental"-looking red tapestry on one wall. In the third season, bachelor Andrew Firestone takes a few of the women to share Ethiopian food, which they eat with their hands off a low table, sitting on the floor in a room decorated with "Middle-Eastern"-looking tapestries. At the end of the meal, they lounge on cushions on the floor and are entertained by belly dancers who encourage the women to dance for Andrew. In the fifth season, bachelor Jesse Palmer takes three women on a date to an opulent tent set outdoors where they are greeted by a live elephant. The set designers deck out the tent in "Middle-Eastern"-looking décor, with gilded red pillows strewn across the floor, gilded red tapestries hanging from the walls, a low table at the center of the room, and "Oriental" rugs layered on the ground. "Middle-Eastern"-sounding music plays in the background. Jesse spends part of the date doing what one might expect in this setting, rolling around and "making-out" with one of the women. Over the course of the date, he kisses all three women, either in the tent or in secluded areas outside. In the tenth season, on the second episode, Andy takes seven of the women on a group date on the Sunset Strip (in Hollywood). The evening begins with Andy sending a bunch of evening gowns to the girls' hotel room. They each select one to wear that evening. The date ends on the rooftop of the swank hotel (adorned with shag carpets, couches, a hot tub, and a pool); the women eventually strip off their gowns to their bikinis, and Andy lounges in the pool with the seven women. In fact, in season six of *The Bachelorette*, the show literally sets up camp in an "exotic" Eastern locale when Ali goes to Istanbul with several of the men. On her date with one of the men, they walk through an open-air market (replete with exotic spices and Turkish delight) and go into a stall that sells clothing. The next scene shows Ali trying on a belly-dancing outfit for her man, while he dons a Sultan hat.

The harem structure is particularly explicit in the sixth season, when bachelor Byron moves into a guest house in the garden behind the bachelorette pad where the women live, giving him unlimited access to the women. On episode four, for example, he organizes a pajama party at the women's house, providing the lingerie for the women to wear. While the women also have access to the bachelor, Byron decides just how much: in the fifth episode, for example, Byron insists that Jayne, who comes to visit him, leave his quarters because, as he tells us in voice-over, he does not want to "complicate" things by having any of the women spend the night. When the bachelor is not present, the activities of the women are staged for the pleasure of "the scopic privilege of the master in an exclusionary space inaccessible to other men" (Shohat and Stam, 1994, p. 164): they navigate the difficulties of living together while they frolic about in bikinis, prance from hot tub to pool, play lawn games, drink lots of alcohol, and, of course, gossip and fight with one another.

The harem décor accentuates the sexual possibilities at the bachelor's disposal and emphasizes that the women are to be ever-ready and willing to make use of the cushy privacy (cameras notwithstanding) afforded by the setting. The space of *The Bachelor* is one where sexual dilettantism is celebrated and explored, part of the Western myth about the Eastern harem, a place of sexual excess, of limitless pleasure for Western men (Alloula, 1986; Ahmed 1982). The bachelor is the Sheik of this realm, the white playboy who has arrived in a dark land to frolic before returning to more serious ventures and to his white leading lady. On the road to finding a mate, the bachelor has numerous opportunities for lusty forays with many women who await the pleasure of being conquered by him.

The permeation of the "Eastern" via the implicit (never explicitly referenced) trope of the harem is emblematic of the way the BI works through both implicit and explicit issues having to do with race: racial diversity frames the central narrative of two white people forming a romantic union. Diversity ultimately works to maintain pedagogies of whiteness, while situating diversity as essential in defining and highlighting whiteness (Gray, 1991; Projansky and Ono, 1999). Although in the Hollywood harem narrative, the East is left far behind once the white couple affirms their love, the Western notion of the Eastern harem is nonetheless integral to their happy union. As Shohat and Stam (1994) contend, "eroticizing the Third World allowed the imperial imaginary to play out its own fantasies of sexual domination" (158). Thus, "an oriental setting . . . provided Hollywood filmmakers with license to expose flesh without risking censorship" (Shohat and Stam, 1994, p. 158), because they could claim that they were simply depicting the rituals of a less civilized culture. The white couple can fully enjoy and partake in the sensual rituals of the East (when in Rome do as the Romans do), while in the end distancing themselves from the very same eroticized culture that enabled them to find each other.

People of color in the BI are part of the backdrop, the setting, of the otherwise white narrative. This becomes quite explicitly apparent in some of the later seasons as the show increasingly travels to other countries. While some of the "exotic" locales do not explicitly fit the Eastern harem trope, they work in a similar fashion: the exotic other highlights the story of two white people falling in love. For instance, on season fourteen of *The Bachelor*, the overnight dates take place in St. Lucia. On his date with Gia, Jake takes her for a walk in downtown St. Lucia (akin to a montage scene in a romantic film when the couple falls in love) where they talk to the locals (who are black) and dance while the locals play reggae music for them and offer them fresh coconut. Thus, while the bachelor may frolic with women of color during his sojourn in the harem and may visit and play in faraway lands with people of color, in the end he leaves the exotic locales and the harem with his chosen white partner.

Women of Color and Romance

There are a few women of color who become romantically involved with the bachelor. Lanease, an African American woman in the first season, is one woman of color shown romantically involved with a bachelor. Lanease is the first woman to kiss bachelor Alex. However, Alex makes clear, in a private confession to the camera, that she was not his first choice for the romantic boat ride (where they kiss). Of the two women competing for the boat ride (by playing blackjack), he wanted the other woman (a white woman) to win. Alex admits, however, that he enjoyed the boat ride. In voice-over, as he kisses Lanease, he describes her as more "cosmopolitan," "savvy," and "intelligent" than the other women. However, these qualities are ultimately irrelevant in terms of her long-term appeal, qualities rarely mentioned by any of the bachelors as desirable in a romantic partner. Lanease is thus characterized by Alex as a fun person to "fool around with," but not necessarily a woman with whom he would choose to settle down.

Lanease is one of two women of color in fourteen seasons who is shown explicitly broaching the topic of the potential difficulty of an interracial relationship. Right before the third rose ceremony, she asks Alex if the fact that they are from different races is an issue for him. Alex responds that it is not an issue and returns the question. She replies that surely they will face some problems, but that she is ready for whatever might happen. Similarly, on the second episode of season twelve, Marshana (African American woman) broaches the same topic with bachelor Matt Grant on a date, asking him where he stands on interracial dating. He responds that he had not thought about it, explaining that he picked her because she is beautiful and insists that the color of her skin is irrelevant. Since the overriding paradigm of the show is assimilationist, it makes sense that the series shows the bachelor giving the question little consideration.

Alex eliminates Lanease on episode three, explaining to the camera, in private, that he did so because she still has feelings for her ex-boyfriend, information he solicits from a competing participant. Lanease therefore violates the harem structure, which dictates that she make herself available only to the bachelor. Lanease has no voice in what the show constructs as the most important reason for her departure, her feelings for her ex. The series shows the confession of this "sin" coming from another woman. Just as the harem structure situates the sexual dalliances of the bachelor, Lanease becomes one (lustful) step on the way to finding a romantic partner.

Although Lanease appears upset when eliminated, she is not seen crying. She tells the camera that if Alex does not feel absolutely certain about them, if he has any doubts, then this was not going to work anyhow. Her nonplussed behavior contrasts with how the series shows most of the white women who were involved with the bachelor responding to being eliminated: tears and emotion. Yet again, the series shows a woman of color behaving differently from what viewers have come to expect from the white women. This is made especially salient on this episode when the series focuses on the response of a white woman, Rhonda, to being eliminated. On the episodes leading up to her elimination, Rhonda is shown spending very little time with Alex. Unlike Lanease, she is not seen alone with him or kissing him. However, Rhonda is shown speaking with emotion about her strong feelings for Alex, something Lanease is never seen doing. At this rose ceremony, Lanease would seemingly have the most to be upset about since, of all the women eliminated, the series shows her having the strongest connection with the bachelor. However, her departure appears anticlimactic. Instead, it is Rhonda's response—an anxiety attack—that provides the climactic moment at the end of the episode: Rhonda struggles for breath and the paramedics arrive to help.

As mentioned earlier, Naomi's race is never identified on season thirteen. According to conventional physical stereotypes, she could be a tanned white woman, a Latina, or a light-skinned mixed race woman (perhaps white and black). It is unclear how we are meant to read her racially. In many ways, she functions as white. Though on the season for six episodes, Naomi remains unremarkable throughout, until just before her elimination. She is not featured in any storylines. Her relationship with Jason is characterized as a slow-growing attraction that develops over several episodes. In this way, Naomi has potential as a final ideal white woman, since these women are often in the background until the very end, at which point they take center stage.

Unfortunately, Naomi's moment in the spotlight has little to do with her growing relationship with Jason. Naomi becomes remarkable by association with her family, her parents, who are presented as very odd and who are, like Naomi, racially ambiguous. Prior to introducing Jason to her parents, Naomi tells him that her parents are divorced and that she does not have a perfect family. The host warns of what's to come when he tells us that after the commercial break we will see one of the "wackiest" hometown visits. During the visit, Hector, Naomi's father, is presented as obsessed with religion, the only thing he talks about throughout the visit. Hector pulls Jason aside not to ask Jason about his feelings for his daughter (what most fathers do in these scenes) but to inquire about Jason's knowledge of Christianity and the importance of it in his life—which is particularly ironic since Jason is Jewish (though this, too, is never explicitly mentioned during the season). Hector tells Jason about the significance of Christianity in his life, affirming that religion helped him rise above his divorce. Naomi's mother, Sabine (not racially marked), is shown only engaging in unusual activities. For instance, she brings out a bunch of hula hoops and insists Jason and the rest of the family practice their hula-hooping skills in the backyard. She also makes Jason officiate at the burial of a bird she killed by accident while driving (which she brought home and stored in the freezer in a brown paper bag). Finally, Sabine pulls Jason aside to talk about her premonitions, to assess what color Jason is (indigo, it turns out), and to ask for Jason's thoughts on reincarnation. In this way, Naomi's father is presented as overly obsessed with Christianity and her mother as unconventionally spiritual.

In the scenes with Naomi's parents, we see shots of Jason alternately laughing and smiling politely and looking awkwardly to the side, cues to viewers that he is uncomfortable. Naomi is presented as embarrassed about the visit, but good-humored. Naomi does, however, tell the camera that she wishes she and

Jason had discussed religion prior to his visit, since it is such a big deal to her father. In the following episode, Jason eliminates Naomi, telling her they are in different places in their lives, looking for different things. However, he makes a point to reassure her that her elimination has nothing to do with her family, further highlighting that her family was unusual and suggesting a connection between a raced (though ambiguously so) subject and a problematic family. This is an especially significant connection for an ambiguously raced subject, since it is through her family (providing the "origin" of her racialization) that she can be racialized (also the case with Mary, as discussed shortly).

What is notable about Naomi's presentation is that she remains on the series for a long time, yet there is little narrative focus on her until the end. This fits some of the ways women of color are presented in the BI, present but insignificant in terms of being part of the central love narrative—except that in Naomi's case there is a budding romantic relationship between her and Jason. As well, Naomi takes up space in the storyline at the point when she is marked as different by association with her parents. It is following this moment that she is eliminated. This latter aspect of her presentation perhaps confirms that she is a woman of color—too different, too foreign for the bachelor, as signified through a father overly obsessed with religion and an esoteric mother.

Channy, a Cambodian woman from season fourteen who is eliminated on the first episode, is also marked as too different for the bachelor. In this case, she is too forward sexually. However, her sexuality is explicitly tied to her racialization. All her moments onscreen as well as all the references to her highlight her Cambodian heritage or her sexual desires—usually both at once, drawing a link between them. Audiences are first introduced to Channy when she greets bachelor Jake by saying something to him in Cambodian and flirtatiously telling him that if he wants to know what she said he should come find her. The next time she appears, she tells the camera that Jake seems like a "good boy," which is fine, she tells us laughingly, since she can be a "naughty girl." Following this, audiences see Channy say to the camera that Jake needs "a little bit of Cambodian fever." Shortly after is a scene with Channy and Jake on a couch, Channy holding Jake's hands. Channy repeats what she said earlier in Cambodian and then translates the sentence into English: "Jake, you can land your plane on my landing strip any time" (safe to assume the "landing strip" she's referring to is the thin strip of hair left on the pubic bone after waxing the bikini area, popularly called a "landing strip").

All of Channy's moments onscreen construct Channy as foreign, exotic, other, and highly sexual. In the audience's first introduction to Channy (and apparently the first time Jake meets her as well), language is an explicit marker of her difference, and what she says in Cambodian is later translated as explicitly sexual, inviting Jake to have sex with her anytime he wants. The comment about "Cambodian fever" exoticizes Channy by suggesting her "Cambodianness" will raise Jake's temperature. Of course, this comment also aligns sexual attraction to Channy with an illness one catches when traveling abroad. Channy's confession that she is willing to be the "naughty girl" is rife with connotations about how she will seduce Jake, leading him away from his good ways.

Channy's sexualized behavior and the attachment of this to her racialization as Cambodian is also the focus of discussions about her between host Chris and Jake. As Chris runs through different women with Jake near the end of the episode, he asks Jake for his impression of Channy, saying, "Let's talk about Channy, who came at you with a little Cambodia." This is an odd turn of phrase, implying that Channy is aggressively attacking the bachelor (coming at him) and suggesting playfully that the attack is akin to a little country coming after him: Cambodia is characterized as a "little country," and Channy's identity stands in for this aggressive little country. Channy, it is also implied by this turn of phrase, is not a U.S. citizen, but rather a representative of a foreign and exotic country. In fact, she literally *is* that country. After this comment by Chris, the scene of Channy speaking to Jake in Cambodian is shown for the second time, with an emphasis on shots of Jake laughing politely and looking uncomfortable as he listens to Channy. To emphasize the discomfort of the scene, this time faint but persistent music with a "tinky" discordant sound plays in the background, alerting the audience that something is off. The scene switches back to Jake and Chris talking. Jake laughs and says, "I was a little speechless, and tried to take it as playful. It was pretty forward." Channy's behavior is presented as making the bachelor uncomfortable, as not entirely welcome. He does his best (but it is work on his part) to see her behavior as playful, but ultimately finds her, in his words, "pretty forward."

Channy is eliminated at the end of the episode. It is worth noting that in this episode some (though not all) of the white women are first introduced to us via a montage of scenes of them in their hometown with a voice-over of the women talking about their lives. As evident from the above, this is not how we are introduced to Channy. As well, once eliminated at the end of the episode, many of the white women are given time onscreen to express their feelings. This is also not the case with Channy. In essence, Channy is not given the space to become a full character with whom we can empathize. By selecting only the clips of Channy described above, the BI explicitly aligns Channy with her racialization as Cambodian and marks her as highly sexual, drawing a connection between these two things and constructing her as different (too sexual) from the other women and as ultimately an unsuitable romantic partner for the bachelor because of this.

Finally, Mary, from season four (who returns in season six), is another woman of color the series shows romantically involved with a bachelor. Mary has more screen time than any other woman of color in the series. In season four, the series constantly portrays Mary in a way that marks her as an "exotic Other" and therefore as an unsuitable match for all-American Bob, but in season six she becomes the perfect match for bachelor Byron. A key factor in her portrayal in each season is how her ethnicity is marked: in season four she is distinguished as Latina, in season six she is not. Like a cipher, Mary can be signified racially according to need. Along similar lines, Tessa from season ten, who is mixed race Asian American (she wins the bachelor's heart in the end), is not identified as Asian American, even though physically she looks mixed race Asian and her mother has Asian features (her father is marked as white). Tessa and Mary are effectively treated as white.

Maaa-rrri-aa: Hot Latina

In season four, Mary is coded in several stereotypical ways for Latinas. She is seen dancing seductively and with abandon, using sexual movements, baring her bottom to Bob in the second episode, and telling the camera that the music just overcame her. She is pictured as very sexual (Valdivia, 2000; López, 1991) and "tropicalized" (abandons herself to the music, excessive in her movements) (Aparicio and Chávez-Silverman, 1997; Shohat, 1991; Shohat and Stam, 1994). Her bottom becomes a focal point (Negrón-Mutaner, 1997; Guzman and Valdivia, 2004). Indeed, season four shows recurring images of Mary's bottom. When she wears a bikini on episode six, her bottom is shown in extreme close-up as she pulls off her robe, and Bob says "Ay Caramba." A scene of Bob and Mary in bathing suits taking a shower follows. Again a close-up shot from behind, with Mary's bottom taking up half the screen and their clasped hands the other half.[4]

Mary's age (thirty-five) also becomes a key part of her characterization in season four. Her biological clock ticks loudly throughout her tenure on the show. Many of her conversations with Bob about their potential future together center on her age and her desire for family. The sexualizing of Mary in this season, coupled with her desire for family and children, fits with stereotypes about "dark" people from "other" countries being fecund and sexual (Ruiz, 2002, p. 4-5; Ono and Sloop 2002, p. 40). Bob ultimately eliminates Mary, saying he is not yet ready to start a family and not sure when or if he ever will be. Interestingly, in season six, when only one side of these qualities about Mary are played up, the desire for family and children, Mary appears as the ideal mate for bachelor Byron (discussed shortly).

Language Barriers, the American Dream, and Becoming White

Language is one important way Mary is marked ethnically and as different from the other (white) women. In the first episode of season four, Mary greets Bob with the words "Olá, Señor." She is often shown whispering softly to Bob in Spanish. On episode two, two of the other women ask Mary to translate a phrase into Spanish for them. Bob usually greets Mary by pronouncing her name with a mock Spanish accent (Maaa-rrri-aa).[5] When Mary brings Bob home to meet her parents, language becomes an even more explicit marker.[6] This scene emphasizes Bob's confusion in trying to converse with Mary's father, who speaks only Spanish. As with Channy in season fourteen, language marks Mary throughout as exotic and different from the other women and from Bob. In Mary's case, her father's inability to speak English turns this difference into a sign of the distance this "difference" will create between Mary (and her family) and Bob, the all-American guy. The inability to speak English fluently is an impregnable barrier on the series. Indeed, in season nine, bachelor Lorenzo Borghese, very drawn to one of the women from Italy (who only speaks Italian), consistently remarks on their inability to communicate and eventually eliminates her because of this communication barrier.

However, in season six, where Byron picks Mary, Spanish is used as a vehicle through which Byron can reach out to Mary's family. In the finale, Byron proposes to Mary in both Spanish and English. He explains in the "After the Final Rose" episode that he did this to let her family know how serious he is about Mary. Language becomes a unifying sign: Byron shows his desire to be a part of Mary's family, to be understood by them and to have her be a part of his life. This time the bachelor's effort to speak a "foreign" language is cast as a goodwill gesture to Mary's family, a sign of his affection (and perhaps his willingness to accept them and their "foreignness"). Mary herself is rarely seen speaking Spanish during this season, suggesting perhaps that she is distanced from her Cuban ethnicity. It is part of her family life, part of her background, but not necessarily an integral part of her day-to-day life.

In contrast to season four, where Mary's "Latina-ness" is played up at every turn, in season six her Cuban ethnicity is only mentioned toward the end. Likewise, Mary's "Americanness" is never at issue in season six, while it is the focus of her characterization in season four. For instance, on episode one of season four, Mary says the show is, for her, the ultimate realization of the "American dream" in terms of romance. She says her family came to the United States to find the "American dream." She confesses to Bob that she loves football and watches it every Saturday. Mary is shown to have fully embraced much of what "America" typically stands for. However, in season four, no matter how much she professes her Americanness, Mary is always—through her language, her body, the way she moves, her desire for children and family, and the obsessive focus of the camera on a particular segment of her body—located as different, "Other," the outsider embracing the "American dream," trying too hard to fit in but never quite succeeding. In season four, while Mary is exotically enticing, ultimately she is simply too different (foreign) to be a lifelong partner for Bob. In the end, the bachelor distances himself from Mary to reaffirm white, Western monogamous love.

Season six of *The Bachelor* also plays out a familiar Hollywood harem trope with Mary. Tracking images of Arabs on the big screen, Shaheen (2001) notes the impact of the Motion Picture Producers and Directors of America Inc. Production Code (1930-1934), which forbid miscegenation in storylines with harem narratives. The code regulated the "unthinkable," that is, "a white Western woman loving a dusky-skinned, swarthy Arab" (Shaheen, 2001, p. 423), and forced filmmakers to find creative ways to explore the Eastern harem narrative and the adventures white Westerners might enjoy in the East. Thus "the fair heroine could love an Arab, provided the robed sheikh turned out to be a Westerner, disguised as an Arab" (Shaheen, 2001, p. 423). In season six of *The Bachelor*, the genders in this trope are reversed. It is Mary who is ultimately revealed to be "whiter" than previously shown (on season four). A significant part of Mary's journey to her union with Byron is overcoming her past heartbreak with Bob. Mary and Byron consistently tell the camera and each other that Mary needs to overcome her experiences with Bob. However, since Mary's presence on season four is marked by her Cuban ethnicity, part of what she has to overcome in season six is this ethnicity. After passing through the dark, mysterious, and sensual realm of the East and overcoming Mary's heartbreaking experiences as an ethnic "other" in Bob's harem, on season six the happy couple's love is confirmed and verified by the discovery of their mutual whiteness. In essence, Mary's journey in the BI is not only that of finding a romantic partner but also of becoming the right kind of woman for this union: "whiter."

Patriotism, Model Minorities, and War Brides

Patriotism emerges as a running theme in the series in season eight (set in Paris) and season nine (set in Italy), both of which romanticize the United States as a different and better country than the one in which the season is set. This theme culminates in season ten with bachelor Andy, a doctor in the navy. The emphasis this season is on Andy's devotion to the navy, his pride in his career, and his gentlemanly virtues. Many of the dates feature navy themes (set on a navy ship, for instance). In line with this portrayal of Andy as among the best America has to offer, the bachelor is intimate with fewer women than previous bachelors.

Andy chooses Tessa in the end, who is mixed race Asian American,[7] activating a familiar trope about Asian Americans as model minorities: a deracialized representation that deemphasizes difference in order to position Asian Americans as model minorities (Osajima, 2005), that is, as an ideal akin to whiteness that other minorities should emulate. The war bride stereotype, an Asian woman who is the ideal middle-class wife, who assimilates perfectly into U.S. life, also comes into play. The war bride is an early version of the model minority, a kind of model of a racialized wife that relies on her being divorced from her larger Asian community (Chung-Simpson, 1998) so she can fully integrate into U.S. life. Tessa is presented as not being part of an Asian community, as divorced from that part of her heritage, since she is never shown mentioning it and since her mom, who physically embodies this part of her background, is virtually invisible during the hometown visit (discussed below). The model mi-

nority and war bride stereotypes work particularly well when coupled with patriotism: the Asian American woman as the ideal and devoted American citizen
who will make a perfect wife. Perhaps foreshadowing this perfect union, these
themes come together when Tina, an Asian American woman (eliminated on
episode five), impresses Andy on the first episode by singing the U.S. national
anthem to him, bringing tears to both their eyes.

As Hardy and I (2008) explain, "there is a fluidity to the category Asian
American that fits the presentation of Tessa as not having a racial identity
(hence, as white) despite visible racial signifiers" (p. 380). While Mary's ethnic
signifiers are visually perhaps mutable, Tessa's are less so. What is remarkable
is that Tessa's ethnicity is never mentioned. Ever. When Tessa brings Andy
home during her hometown visit, her mother (who is physically marked as
Asian, more so than Tessa) is not a main player in the action. This serves to
foreclose any focus on Tessa's Asianness as well as to reify stereotypes about
quiet, demure, and compliant Asian and Asian American women—the "lotus
blossom" or "madame butterfly" stereotype of Asian women (Ono and Pham,
2008, pp. 66-68), minus the sexual allure since the mother is not sexualized. The
treatment of Tessa's mother is unusual, since mothers generally take center stage
during the hometown visits. While Tessa's father, who is marked as white,
occupies a bit more space than her mother, it is Tessa's sister (also mixed race
Asian) and Tessa's best friend (white) who are given the most time on-camera.

While Tessa is treated as white, her Asianness seeps through via her physical features and her mother's presence, working to shore up ideas about what it
means to be a good U.S. citizen and, in this case, a good mate for patriotic navy
officer Andy. The stereotypes about hardworking and dedicated Asians (Wang,
2010) work particularly well here. Patriotism and the model minority myth are
interanimated, with Tessa standing in for the accomplishments that minorities, if
they work hard enough, can achieve in the United States. Tessa's achievement is
landing herself a man of honor who serves his country with pride.

Possibilities for Rupture?

One woman of color threatens to rupture the racist structure of the BI. Anindita,
the South Asian American woman discussed earlier, provides a poignant, funny,
and keenly insightful critique of the series.[8] However, Anindita is never a serious contender for the bachelor's affections. It is in fact curious that Anindita is
given so much screen time in the series. Anindita tells Aaron, before the first
rose ceremony, that the show's process reminds her of something she saw on a
farm: a bull in a trailer surrounded by cows drawn to his smell. She likens the
women on the show to those cows and Aaron to the bull. Anindita challenges
the show by equating humans and animals. She also makes explicit the inherent
male privilege of the setup and the desperate, absurd, and crass situation in
which the women are placed. Furthermore, on "The Women Tell All" episode,

Anindita responds to the host's accusation that she was a troublemaker by saying that while she is being accused of making trouble, the bachelor had "his tongue in two girls' mouths" on one date. Here, Anindita explicitly criticizes the sexual gallivanting and vulgarity afforded by the harem structure.

Anindita also calls attention to how the series is like an arranged marriage. When Anindita is introduced on the first episode of the series, she explains that the reason she wants to be there is that in her culture (she does not specify further) a woman who is twenty-seven and unmarried is like a "going out-of-business sale"—a predicament not exclusive to her culture, since all women in the series (many in their early and midtwenties) appear desperate to be married. Anindita asserts that her background gives her some perspective on the situation, since her parents were the product of an arranged marriage. She says this situation is like an updated version of an arranged marriage. It is worth noting that arranged marriage, like the harem, is a reviled tradition in the West that is used to good effect in the series.

While Anindita seems prepared to accept the setup of the series as one she is familiar with, she can also be considered as ultimately refusing the racist premises of the series, opening up the possibility for a resistant reading and providing pleasure for a resistant reader. Despite the series' attempt to position women of color on the periphery, Anindita provides the possibility for rupture of the hegemonic imperative of white heterosexual romance, male privilege and superiority, and the artifice of reality television. Her positioning as an illegitimate suitor for the bachelor can be read as a challenge to the dominant white masculine pleasures central to the show. In refusing this setup (she decides to leave) but remaining a strong presence, Anindita creates an alternate space in which she need not signify within these oppressive terms. Anindita's characterization is rare for South Asians in popular U.S. media: an intelligent, attractive woman picking away in a witty manner at the racist premise of a television series.

Considering Anindita's biting (though humorous) critique of the series and the threat of her comments upending the ideological premises of the show, it is worth exploring why the makers of the series decided that including her comments would not undermine the show's modus operandi. Because Anindita is never situated as a legitimate romantic partner for the bachelor (she simply does not signify as a romantic partner at all), she falls outside the central paradigms of the show. Her voice is not significant in terms of rupturing the central narrative. The series can therefore include Anindita's comments to offer comic relief and add spice (hooks, 1992, p. 157). Nonetheless, the series does not completely close down the moments of hegemonic rupture afforded by Anindita's comments. Hence, the depiction of Anindita suggests the potential radical resistance women of color can represent on the show (Anindita is dark-skinned, visually marked as a woman of color), even as it simultaneously justifies the choice of a white woman as the only viable suitor.

Leaving the Harem Behind

The sexual gallivanting of the bachelor is "otherized" within the larger romance narrative of the series. The bachelor is to use this time to sow his wild oats with the express purpose of settling down with one woman at the end, presumably in a home with a white picket fence and very few Persian carpets or red pillows— and certainly no elephant grazing on the front lawn. Male protagonists in *The Bachelor*, like the protagonists in classic Hollywood harem films, explore the evils of the Westernized version of the Eastern harem before overcoming these excesses in the interest of sustaining a monogamous union. The bachelors transgress Western monogamous norms via the trope of the Western version of the Eastern harem in order to reaffirm Western norms. A romantic union for a white man can only be found with one white woman; being in love means not lusting after others. The harem experience and the women who are part of this process are, to some extent, the grotesque but necessary other (Stallybrass and White, 1986).

Just as the harem narrative is embedded in the Western narrative of monogamous love, so are portrayals of people of color embedded in the defining of whiteness. Through the trope of the Eastern harem, *The Bachelor*'s racist and imperialist structure tells a story about the romantic heterosexual union of two white people, one that relies on the myth of white man's ability to conquer the dark "other" to find his way toward the ideal white mate. While all women in the series participate in the Orientalist setup, the women of color and the white women serve different purposes. White women can rise above the harem structure to become the bachelor's chosen woman, for whom he will forsake the pleasures of the harem, but unless they can be whitened, women of color cannot.

By placing the harem structure in the United States (in Hollywood the harem remains in the East, but in the end the white couple returns to the West), the series reinscribes not only imperialist desires but also the historical power dynamic of slavery in the United States. Given the history of slavery in the United States and the relationship of women of color to their white masters—as sexual slaves, as mothers to their illegitimate children, but never as legitimate romantic partners (wives) or as equal citizens—the positioning of women of color in *The Bachelor* is particularly disturbing. Here again, women of color fulfill the time-worn roles of satisfying the sexual desires of white men and taking care of white men (by highlighting the inappropriate and potentially dangerous behaviors of white women who want to marry white men). The BI tells a very specific story about whiteness, where whiteness is essential to finding a romantic partner. Once women of color help the white heroes find one another, they must disappear into the background—just as the harem structure disappears to let the white master and his chosen mistress take center stage.

Notes

1.   It is worth noting that there are almost no men of color in any of the seasons of *The Bachelorette*.

2.   Jason Mesnick, star of season thirteen of *The Bachelor*, is reportedly Jewish. However, this is never mentioned on the series. When Jason meets Naomi's family, her father impresses upon him the importance of Christianity and asks Jason to think about the importance of Jesus. The series shows Jason's response in a close-up of a blank stare. Shortly after, Naomi tells Jason that while she is spiritual, she does not care if they do not share the same religion. In this way, it is implied that Jason is not Christian.

3.   Ali chooses Roberto Martinez as her final man. He is Latino, and marked as such throughout (fellow-participants call him "rico suave," his parents speak with an accent and salsa dance when Ali visits).

4.   Most of the women appear in bikinis at some point, with close-ups of their bodies, but Mary is the only one this season for whom the core visual motif is her bottom.

5.   Ono (2000) notes in *Buffy The Vampire Slayer* how the use of a mock accent to communicate with a person who speaks a different language and is from a different culture becomes an exercise in xenophobia (p. 172-177).

6.   In season three, when Andrew goes home to meet Christina's parents (one of the final four women), we find out she is Portuguese. This is the first time her ethnicity is mentioned. She tells Andrew she wants to take him home to give him a taste of her culture and brings him to a Portuguese bakery. He does not like the food. He says to the camera, in private, that during dinner at her family's home he might have to sneak out to get a burger. Christina is eliminated at the end of this episode.

7.   As well, it is important to note the long history of U.S. army men having sexual relations with Asian women while stationed in Asian countries (Feng Sun, 2003). There is also the famous opera (and film) *Madam Butterfly* that configures this setup as a love story.

8.   While some women complain about being unfairly treated by the bachelor or by the other women, only a few women critique the unfair setup of the series.

Chapter 3: Emotional Failure

Building on arguments in Chapter 1 about authenticating and naturalizing the display of emotion in the BI, this chapter and the following one focus specifically on the requirements for emotional behavior: how much emotion a woman should display and the risk in not abiding by the required economy. This chapter also looks at the association in the BI between a woman's ability to be emotionally vulnerable, to show emotion, and her readiness to take the necessary risk to find love. The importance of showing the right economy of emotion applies generally to the white women in the BI, because this is a quality necessary for finding love and women of color are not presented as viable candidates for romance in this context.

There are two dangerous extremes in this economy of emotion (not showing enough emotion or showing too much), and few women achieve the proper balance. Heather, in the example in Chapter 1, exceeds the economy, thus verifying that she is the wrong kind of woman for the bachelor. With her sobbing exclamations and tear-stained face, Heather has the most air time of the ten rejected women in this episode. She signifies the unhappy result of the rose ceremony, poignantly personifying one type of woman to whom the bachelor will not offer a rose: one not in control of her emotions, who responds with too much emotion to situations that do not seem to warrant such a response (she just met the bachelor!). But of course, it is upon women like Heather that the series relies to tell its story (the focus of Chapter 4). This short chapter looks at the women who do not show enough emotion. The tenure of these women is usually short-lived, and if they remain for a few episodes, they are in the background most of the time. The central concern with these women is their seeming inability to open up and take the risk necessary to find love.

Risk for Love

Taking the risk of showing one's emotions under surveillance, and appearing authentic while doing so, works in the BI as both proof of a woman's desire for love and a testimony to the realness of her emotions. Participants regularly invoke their ability to take the risk of being emotionally vulnerable as evidence of their commitment to finding love. Overcoming surveillance, appearing natural under surveillance, is not only important in authenticating a participant, it is also part of the show of bravery required, proof of the ability of a woman (and of most of the men as well) to take the necessary risk that verifies her readiness to find love.

For example, Jillian, star of season five of *The Bachelorette* (and a participant on season thirteen of *The Bachelor*), talks about her preparedness for being on the series in the first episode, saying to Chris that she's ready to make herself vulnerable, to open her heart and take the risk required to find love. She affirms that the only way to find love is to take a leap of faith and not be constrained by rules (which she admits she had too many of when she appeared on *The Bachelor*). In other words, Jillian needs to be guided by her emotions and not shy away from them, avoiding anything that might limit her ability to be in touch with her feelings. As well, Jason, star of season thirteen of *The Bachelor*, tells viewers in episode one that though he's been hurt twice already, he's willing to take the risk yet again and find love on the series. Love is presented as a process that is painful, requiring one to be open emotionally and to take the risk of being hurt.

In fact, emotional vulnerability is the final obstacle participants need to overcome at some point during the last three dates (overnight dates, meeting the family, final date). In the final few episodes, the remaining participants (male and female) all have a "watershed moment" where they lay their cards on the table and tell the star their feelings. This is always framed as a risk they finally decide to take, with some trepidation (but with absolute conviction), once they realize they need to be completely open about their feelings to have any hope of winning the star's heart. Usually prior to this moment the star has mentioned sensing barriers in the other person, barriers that are removed as soon as the participant takes the risk of confessing his or her feelings. For example, Jason on season thirteen of *The Bachelor*, on episode seven (the overnight dates), says of Molly (the woman he later marries) that he feels like he has to pull a lot of things out of her. She is not forthcoming about her feelings. Then we see Molly telling Jason that she has had walls up, has not made herself vulnerable to him, but that she is ready to do so now even though she is afraid. She tells Jason she is falling in love with him, that she wants to be there on the show. Following this scene, viewers hear Jason say in voice-over, as Molly and Jason kiss onscreen, that he needed to hear this from her, and that everything changed once she told him her feelings. Next shot is of Molly telling the camera that they had a break-through, that she needed to be emotional.

Taking a risk for love is an ongoing problem for Ali and part of the story-line on season six of *The Bachelorette*. Right before the rose ceremony on epi-sode five (already well into the action at this point), Chris and Ali sit down to talk. Chris tells Ali that she is afraid to let herself fall in love and that she needs to get over this. Ali tells him she is going to be very cautious when it comes to her heart, explaining that she does not want to get hurt. Chris says she can't go through this process carrying that fear, that she must let it go, that she needs to take a leap of faith for love, that she must trust her instincts. Of course, Ali is eventually shown doing exactly this, letting her walls down so she can fall for Roberto, her final chosen man.

Withholding Emotion

Many women are not able to open up enough emotionally to remain on the se-ries, that is, enough to show they are willing to take the risk necessary to find love. Haily, from season two of *The Bachelor*, fails miserably at this task. On the fourth episode, Aaron (the bachelor for season two) and Haily are on a group date in a sailboat on a sunny day. In medium close-up shot, Aaron is alone as he says to the camera that he wishes Haily wasn't so afraid of opening up, express-ing his desire for her to be herself and to "quit being so concerned about not being herself." Then we are shown a medium close-up of Haily and Aaron hold-ing onto the railing of a sailboat, Haily with a sun hat partially covering her face, holding her head down, and Aaron looking toward her. They have an exchange about taking risks to find love, a constant preoccupation in the BI. Both are con-cerned Haily is not willing to take the emotional risk needed. Haily lifts her head and tells Aaron she's unsure why this is so hard, but she thinks it's because she's afraid of being too vulnerable. Aaron asks, as she looks down again, "Is it a risk worth taking?" She looks at him and replies that there are certain risks that are more frightening than others, especially ones that concern the heart. At the end of this episode, Haily does not receive a rose. Aaron tells the camera that he doesn't know her well enough to keep her on the series.

As I have said throughout, the series is edited to tell a particular story, so there is no way of knowing what transpired between Aaron and Haily. We only get the edited version. In looking at the story told about Haily, we can surmise that the makers of the series privilege one reading of Haily's behavior among several possible readings: as unwilling to share herself with Aaron and thus as an unsuitable romantic heroine, because she cannot confess her emotions for the camera. Haily is not constructed as devoid of emotion but rather as filled with emotions that frighten her, that she fears will make her vulnerable if revealed. Reading how Aaron's actions are presented is telling in terms of the type of woman the series constructs as suitable for the star (assuming Aaron's actions are edited to tell a particular story about the star), as well as what Aaron imagines is Haily's potential for being that woman. Presenting Aaron as wanting Haily to be open and herself suggests there is a real self she can be, that she should be, that he (or the series, in actuality) wishes she would be—but that she is not being. Aaron is shown having in mind a specific kind of Haily he wants to get to know, and this Haily is, he suggests, the genuine real Haily, the one she is refusing to reveal. The problem seems to be Haily's unwillingness to show her real self, and this real self (so Aaron imagines) is the woman he is looking for as a partner. This real Haily, the one in hiding, is not afraid to show her emotions in a contrived setting under surveillance, one imagines, and is willing to take the necessary risk to find love. In other words, authentic selves are ones who are willing to show their emotions under surveillance, especially in the name of love. The BI constructs Haily's problem as an inability to open up and show who she really is (the call to authenticity is a call to reveal what is naturally already there, and it is also a call to whiteness, as discussed in Chapter 1).

Aaron reads Haily's behavior as demonstrating her unwillingness to open up and reveal her real and genuine self, and consequently as showing an unwillingness to take the risk necessary to find love. In this sense, Haily's behavior is also cast as willful: she purposefully, out of fear, hides her real self (i.e., her emotional self). She does this because, as Aaron's comments suggest, she is not comfortable enough with herself to be herself—she does not want to be vulnerable and show her real feelings. Haily's supposed inability to reveal her true self becomes not only a lack of comfort with herself but also a lack of courage. She is not ready to take the risk necessary to find love. This reading of Haily is confirmed not only by Aaron (when he eliminates her), but also by how the series constructs Haily's assessment of her own behavior when she says she does not know why this is so hard and admits she is afraid of being vulnerable.

It is worth considering alternate explanations for Haily's seeming withholding behavior. This line of thinking, a kind of "what if" scenario, provides insight into how the BI privileges one way of being over another, how it makes things make sense. Assuming Haily is withholding, maybe she does not want to open up because she is not interested in Aaron. Maybe it is less a question of her not opening up and more that what she has revealed shows her to be the type of woman Aaron does not want to be with, that is, someone who does not wear her heart (emotions) on her sleeve. Or perhaps Haily's discomfort is about the show's premise that love can be found in this type of context. Or maybe she is simply not willing to show her emotions in front of a camera. My point is that Haily's behavior is configured as specifically related to her suitability for love, as an unwillingness to be emotionally vulnerable in order to find love. She is also presented as full of emotions (rather than devoid of emotions) but afraid to let them out.

Aaron encounters similar difficulties with the fourth runner-up, Angela. However, the problem with Angela is that she may actually not have emotions, a fate far worse than Haily's withholding of emotion. Aaron eliminates Angela in episode five. As they hug after the rose ceremony in which she is eliminated, Aaron tells her how difficult it is for him to say good-bye to her. Angela, however, says to him in a rather sprightly voice as she is about to get into the limousine, "have fun." Once Angela is inside the limousine, her face is shown in close-up, and unlike most participants who at this point declare their heartbreak, express regret that the star did not get to see the "real me" (or the star would surely have fallen in love with them), or profess that this has been an incredible learning experience, Angela says:

> I wish that I could have been different with Aaron and more relaxed, but I wasn't. It's hard for me to believe that you can really be in love and that that person will love you forever, but I don't want to be numb. I don't want to be that way. I'm not used to affection. I'm not used to saying what I feel. That's what I worry about, that I'm going to be forty and alone. I don't want to be like that. That's what I think about. I think about it every night before I go to bed, that I don't want to be this way. I pray that I'm not the cold-hearted bitch that I sometimes think I am.

Several things are notable. Angela expresses keen insight into the requirements on the BI: to appear relaxed (similar to what Nikki expresses in the example in Chapter 1 about appearing natural on the series), to show emotion, to be affectionate, believe in a romantic notion of love, and have the ability to commit immediately to a life with another person. She acknowledges her uncertainty and her inability to enact these things, showing a sharp awareness that an inability to properly perform the required behavior will reveal her true and genuine self to be cold, numb, impenetrable, and withholding.

Given the ethos of the series, if love can only be found between people who are willing to open up immediately about their feelings, then Angela's inability to "open up" effectively disqualifies her from the race as the BI has set it up. Unlike Haily, it is not Angela's inability to take a leap of faith that damns her, but her lack of faith in the premise of finding love on the BI. It is what she *does* reveal (she is cold and devoid of emotion), rather than what she has been unable to reveal (the problem with Haily). This makes Angela particularly troubling— almost unnatural in the space of the BI—since underlying the construction of white women in the space of the BI is the assumption that they are always emotional. The variables are their willingness to display these emotions (as we see with Haily) and their ability to control them (discussed in the following chapter). As detailed in Chapter 1, women are meant to naturally reveal their authentic selves, which revolves around showing their emotions in appropriate ways.

What makes Angela sympathetic, however, is her sadness at her inability to enact what is required of her and her desire to do so. She speaks of her concern over what will happen to her if she fails to feel the appropriate emotions. Unfortunately for Angela, her friend Summer (also her roommate), a main player in the storyline during the visit to Angela's hometown, is of no help in Angela's endeavor to find love. Summer defies almost all the promoted emotional and authenticating behaviors sanctioned on the BI. Summer does not "make sense" within the BI, or rather she only makes sense as odd, mean, and irrational, an outsider to what is deemed appropriate and desirable behavior. The association of Summer with Angela emphasizes that Angela's behavior is to be read as unusual, marking Angela as an unviable candidate for love on the BI and further highlighting the need to show emotion in prescribed ways for the sake of love.

The setup of the visit with Summer is unique in the BI. During the episode when participants bring the star to their hometown to meet their family, it is common for friends and extended family members to be present but rare for them to have as much air time as Summer is given (unless the parents are unable to meet the star, which is not the case with Angela). Generally the focus is on immediate family. Although Angela introduces Aaron to her family, the focus here is on the visit with Summer. During visits, family members (especially parents) are sometimes critical of the imperatives of the series, of the push to develop real feelings in such a short time and in a contrived setting—especially of the pressure to become engaged and marry quickly. This verifies that the families are loving and concerned about their children. Usually these concerns are smoothed over when the children reassure their parents of their intense feelings for the star and their readiness for what lies ahead. As Angela's friend (not her family), Summer is not a legitimate person to be raising these issues, and so her concerns are presented as illegitimate as well. She is framed as questioning the imperatives of the series not out of concern for Angela but because of her own problems with love, her inability to be a good friend to Angela, and ultimately, her irrationality.

The scene I examine takes place in the living room of Angela and Summer's apartment. Just prior to the meeting with Summer, Aaron confesses to the camera that Angela warned him about her roommate, telling him Summer is a little strange. He admits he is a bit nervous about meeting her. This statement suggests apprehensiveness about what is to follow, and about Summer in particular. As Angela and Aaron enter the room to meet Summer, the camera is handheld, suggesting they have entered an unpredictable, unsteady space, a space where they need to be on their toes because anything can happen. Throughout the scene, Summer's face remains motionless as she looks straight ahead, while Angela and Aaron's faces move around within the shots (they look sideways at each other, or look down). The editing and mise-en-scène suggest Summer is in the position of interrogator, a stance that makes Aaron and Angela very uncomfortable. Part of what makes Summer's characterization disconcerting is that the types of questions she poses and her demeanor are usually reserved for fathers on the series. Generally only family members, and only some of them (the parents), interrogate in this manner. Summer takes on a role she does not, within the logic of the series, have the authority to play, which further situates her queries as misguided, out-of-place, and inappropriate.

Below is a transcription of a lengthy piece of dialogue, as it provides an overall sense of the flow of the exchange. Most of the scene alternates between medium close-up shots of Summer sitting on a chair petting a dog,[1] and medium close-up, close-up, and medium long shots of Angela and Aaron sitting on a couch across from Summer. The shots suggest this is both an intimate and an uncomfortable situation. The musical motif interspersed throughout the scene is a faint, low-pitched, short, fast "da-da-da-da . . ." on a keyboard, heightening the sense of discomfort.

Summer:	So, why did you keep Angela along? (musical motif in background)
Aaron:	She's been a bit mystical. She's been a real dark horse, soft-spoken and quiet and shy.
Summer:	So, what is different about her from the other girls?
Aaron:	She seems like a real person. She seems real genuine. She's not catty. She's not vindictive whatever.
Summer:	Oh, you don't know her.
Summer:	Your face is the color of this couch (to Angela). I'm kidding (to Angela).

At this point, the scene cuts to a medium shot of Angela in a room alone confessing to the camera: "When we first started talking, I could tell he was real uncomfortable" (the musical motif returns in the background). Then another shot of the living room with Angela, Summer, and Aaron. Summer is asking them about how the experience has been so far on the series. The following exchange takes place:

Summer:	Well, you guys started getting uncomfortable when I started asking what you think of her.
Aaron:	She's been real hard to get to know, real hard. I mean, everyone else spoke highly of her.
Summer:	Would you have picked her if everyone else didn't speak highly of her. . .

Aaron responds by saying no, he wouldn't have. Summer says "so you just based it on your friends' opinions?" At this point, Aaron begins telling Summer that he hasn't met Angela's family yet, which he thinks will be important in finding out more about her. Summer is not interested in pursuing this line of conversation and says:

Summer:	You didn't really answer my question. So, what are you going to base it on (musical motif returns, louder and more pronounced)?
Aaron:	Well, initially? Well, you've got to have some physical attraction, or you're not gonna want to talk to them . . . but beyond that, you've got to know . . .

Summer: So, you are superficial? No, I'm just kidding. I'm just kidding. I
               have a question for you (to Angela). So if he proposed, what
               would you say?

Angela responds by saying she isn't sure what she would say to a proposal.
Summer interjects with "that's a romantic answer." Aaron comes to Angela's
rescue at this point, stating that he doesn't expect Angela to know the answer to
that question. Summer asks Aaron if he thinks any of the remaining four girls
would say yes to a proposal? Aaron tells her he does. At this point, Summer
turns to Angela and asks if this fact concerns her.

The use of the recurring musical motif, first heard when Summer asks
Aaron why he kept Angela on the show, inspires apprehension about Summer.
This same musical motif returns as Angela tells the camera (in private) that she
could tell Aaron was really uncomfortable during the meeting. The series plays
the musical motif a final time when Summer repeats the same question to Aaron
for the third time (why he kept Angela), insisting that Aaron has not adequately
answered her question.[2] This time the music increases in volume, more pronounced and insistent. The music warns that Summer's presence is threatening
and is becoming more menacing as the exchange progresses—reminiscent of the
musical motif in the series of *Jaws* films, which warns of the approach of the
shark and increases in intensity as the shark nears. Coupled with the musical
motif is the recurring image of Summer slowly petting a dog who sits at her feet:
Summer remains calm and collected as her guests become agitated.

Aaron, in response to Summer's question of why he kept Angela (faint musical motif in the background indicating that danger is associated with the question), explains by characterizing Angela as "a bit mystical," "a real dark horse,"
"soft-spoken," "quiet and shy," "not catty," "not vindictive." Summer is un-
swayed by his answers and asks him to specify what differentiates Angela from
the other women. Aaron tries to elaborate, using tried and true paradigms on the
series: he kept Angela because she is "real" and "genuine." Summer remains
unimpressed with this answer, and at this point Aaron becomes quite uncomfortable, indicated by the use of close-up shots of his face and shots of him looking
down or to the side each time he finishes a sentence. If this were not enough to
indicate his discomfort, the scene is intercut with a medium close-up of Angela
(from a private interview after the encounter) telling the camera that she could
tell Aaron was "real uncomfortable."

At this point in the exchange, the musical motif returns faintly in the background, warning of what is next and further justifying Aaron's discomfort (the
villainess is closing in on the hero). Aaron appears flustered throughout, but
more so toward the end of the exchange as he alternates between repetitive and
monosyllabic answers. Meanwhile, the series shows Summer in medium shots
and a few low-angle shots and tilt-ups (from her hand petting the dog up to her
face) calmly repeating the same questions as she pets her dog. At one point,
Summer is shown in a medium handheld shot, and the effect, as with the use of

the handheld camera at the beginning of the scene, is to make her presence disconcerting, unsteady, menacing.

Not only does Summer discount Aaron's qualification of Angela as real and genuine (to which she jokingly and sarcastically suggests he doesn't know her), she pointedly comments on Aaron and Angela's discomfort when she asks him his thoughts about Angela. This comment pushes the conversation outside the language of emotion and insists on a metanarrative about how their bodily behavior betrays their feelings. This is also a meta-discussion about the requirements of the series when it comes to emotional behavior and love, with Summer's comments suggesting these requirements are not quite as natural in the pursuit of love as the BI constructs them. At this point, Aaron is shown frustrated and lost. This is mirrored in the use of a quick long shot from behind Angela and Aaron sitting on the couch, suggesting that this incident is moving the action farther and farther away from the central explicit goal and important action of the series, finding love. Aaron's discomfort is reflected in the aesthetics of the scene through an awkward camera angle that elicits discomfort in viewers.

Aaron admits to Summer that he has found it difficult to get to know Angela but adds that other people liked her. Summer challenges him by asking if he would have selected her if this were not the case. At this point, Aaron gives an answer he seems reluctant to give, almost out of exasperation, admitting he would not have chosen Angela if that were not the case. As he answers, there is a close-up of his face looking straight at Summer and then down at the ground. Summer responds by pressing the issue further, asking if he chose Angela based on the opinions of others. When Aaron still fails to give a satisfactory answer, she points this out to him by saying he hasn't answered her question and insists he do so. At this point, the musical motif returns, but this time loud and pronounced, letting viewers know that the imminent danger we have been anticipating has finally arrived. Aaron's discomfort is magnified through a close-up of his face and then a zoom into an even closer shot of his face as he tries to answer her question. He appears at once earnest, struggling to answer, and very uncomfortable.

Summer finally tires of her line of questioning and begins to more explicitly address the setup of the series. She asks Angela what she would do if Aaron were to propose. When Angela responds that she doesn't know, Summer exclaims that her answer isn't very romantic. Immediately after this exchange, we see Summer saying to the camera (while she is alone) that she would advise Angela to turn down a proposal from Aaron, because she (Summer) is extremely skeptical of marriage. She continues, saying it is not possible to fall in love and commit to marriage within the space of six weeks. These statements make it clear Summer does not think the setup of the series is conducive to finding love, or even romance. Summer also raises questions about the appropriateness of the harem structure of the series for finding love when she asks Angela if the fact that some of the other women would already say yes to a proposal concerns her.

As Aaron and Angela leave the apartment, we hear Aaron say in voice-over that the questions from Summer were unlike any he has been asked so far.[3] He asserts that he has never met anyone like Summer, that she is very apprehensive about everything, and that she seems to want to prevent Angela from getting to know him. This is the first time Aaron has been confronted with someone who is adamantly unwilling to go along with the premise of the series, unwilling to use the prescribed language of emotion, and unwilling (unlike Haily and Angela) to admit this as a failing on her part. In fact, this is the first time anyone in the BI exhibits this behavior.

One has to wonder why, considering the circumstances, Aaron (or any of the other starring bachelors or bachelorettes) is not confronted more often by such pointed questions. Taking Summer's questions seriously, rather than taking Aaron's side and dismissing them as unreasonable, a few things emerge: how well does Aaron know Angela? Has it been difficult for him to get to know her? Did he pick her to remain on the series only because others spoke highly of her? All of these things, one might think, are important in determining Aaron's character as well as his feelings for Angela. For the sake of making explicit the behaviors privileged within the space of the BI, I ask: why does the construction of Summer as the villainess supersede the representation of Aaron as shallow? Or as not knowing Angela very well? Or, of the series as an untenable way to find true love? Why do Summer's concerns have no currency in relation to the central explicit purpose of the series: finding love?

The only way to make Aaron a sympathetic character in this context and the series a rational space in which to find love, is to characterize Summer as having an agenda that runs counter to the love narrative of the series. As Aaron and Angela drive away from the apartment in a limousine, Angela tells Aaron that Summer always sabotages things, especially love. Aaron warns her to be careful of Summer. Summer's characterization is now complete. She poses a threat (to the values of the show when it comes to love, to her roommate, and to the bachelor), and she will interfere with the natural and legitimate process of falling in love. Angela's apprehension about her friend's intentions and Aaron's warning that she should be cautious about these seal the deal. Further, Aaron and Angela's characterization of Summer situates Summer's concerns as illegitimate, since she is presented as not believing in love and her main purpose as sabotaging anyone who does. This also puts a particular spin on Aaron's failure to answer Summer's persistent questions. It is not a failing on his part but rather a result of his stress at being placed in such a difficult situation, a reasonable response to Summer's mean-spirited attempt to derail the process of finding love.

In the final analysis, Aaron's dumbfounded state when faced with Summer's inquiries is legitimated, and Summer's concerns are constructed as outside the bounds of what is to occur in the process of finding love on the series. Summer and her concerns become a sign of deviance. The pursuit of true love and the confession of emotions are ultimately upheld as worthy, legitimate, and, at times, maligned virtues without which one will end up like Summer, a mean-spirited saboteur.

Angela is, predictably, eliminated in the following episode. The fact of having made it this far on the series suggests there is hope for Angela: she has the potential to find love, provided she can begin to feel the appropriate emotions, believe in the necessity of taking a leap of faith to find love. However, Summer works not only to reify the necessity of the required emotional behavior in the BI but also as a warning of the type of woman Angela could become, and more generally, a warning for all women who question the imperatives about love and emotional behavior set out in the BI.

Notes

1.   Perhaps this is pushing the analogy, but this scene is reminiscent of the villain, Ernst Stavro Blofeld, in several of the *James Bond* films, who is always seen calmly stroking a cat on his lap (a trope made more salient when spoofed in the popular *Austin Powers* films).

2.   Summer can perhaps be seen as occupying the role of therapist or psychiatrist, with her positioning in a separate chair on one side of the couch where Angela and Aaron sit and her steady gaze and persistent line of questioning. This reading certainly fits with the formal cinematic elements as well as the narrative content of the scene, especially with the portrayal of Summer as calm and determined to question Aaron.

3.   Chapter 4 examines Christi from season two and Lee-Ann from season five of *The Bachelor*, who both explicitly question the setup of the series. There is often one woman in a given season of *The Bachelor* who questions the setup of the series, but there are none, other than Summer, who reject its paradigms entirely.

Chapter 4: Excessive Emotion:
Her Money Shot

As discussed in Chapter 3, revelation of an inner, emotional, private self is necessary for survival in the BI, since failure to reveal in this way constructs a participant as unable to open up, unwilling to take the risk required to find love, or more dangerously, in rare cases, as having no emotions. But this emotional revelation carries risks. It is only positive if what is revealed appears consistent with how a woman was originally presented and with how the series shows a woman wanting to present herself. Nonetheless, the BI (and many reality shows) thrives on the display of emotional women, who are responsible for many of its most memorable moments. As host Chris says in the "Women Tell All" episode for season thirteen of *The Bachelor*, when you have twenty-five beautiful, seemingly normal women and you throw in a bachelor, the drama is sure to start. In essence, drama, as enacted by the women, is woven into the very setup of the series. It is the expected outcome.

This chapter looks at women who exceed the required economy of emotion and at what is at stake for them in their quest for love. The women shown in this way are all white, because these are the women who have a shot at love in the BI (and who can therefore also lose this opportunity). One of the most important aspects of women shown as excessively emotional is the contrast between how appealing the woman at first appears and how she unravels over time, becoming undone before our eyes (the suggestion is she unravels before the bachelor's eyes as well). This chapter asks: How does this type of portrayal position women? What is the role of surveillance in this setup?

I begin with an example from the special "Aaron and Helene Tell All," aired shortly after the season finale of the second season of *The Bachelor* (at the end of which bachelor Aaron selects Helene Eksterowicz as his mate). Not only is it difficult to tell why Aaron and Helene break up from the few details provided by the special, but, as with all the action in the BI, this special is one version of what happened, the one constructed by the creators of the show about the breakup. The most striking aspect of the special is Helene's inability to control her emotions throughout.

The host of the special holds separate interviews with Aaron and Helene. During her interview, Helene tells Chris that the last time she was with Aaron, an hour before he got on a plane and left her, he shocked her by telling her his feelings for her were gone. Her eyes begin to tear up as the camera moves into a close-up of her face, and then she begins to cry. Tearfully, she says she never got an explanation for what happened, that the whole thing was completely unexpected. Shortly after this exchange, Chris asks Helene if she still loves Aaron. She tells him she can't switch her feelings on and off quickly, so she can't say she doesn't love him anymore. Again, she breaks down in tears, the camera fixed on her as she leans over to get a tissue. Tissue in hand, she bows her head to cry, the camera moving in once more for a close-up. Chris puts his hand on her knee and tells her to take her time. The scene ends with Helene crying, her head in her hands.

This scene contrasts with how Helene is presented on the series proper, and the contrast is foregrounded in the special. At the beginning of the interview with Aaron, the host asks Aaron to go back to the first night he met Helene, when he told the host that Helene had his attention immediately. Then a close-up of Aaron as he says "I was very impressed with her. She's a very intelligent lady, and we all know she's beautiful. She's got a lot of things going for her. So, in the very beginning, I was extremely impressed with her." Chris asks if the fact that Helene was always playing a bit hard to get attracted him to her. Aaron laughs a bit as he responds that he's always fallen for that kind of woman, fallen into the trap of running after the woman who is a challenge. However, he affirms he was mostly very impressed with Helene overall and that their time together was a lot of fun.

A little later in the interview, the host shows Aaron two clips of Helene (we do not see any clips of Aaron during Helene's interview). In both she is crying. The host asks Aaron how he feels seeing the clips. Aaron says "yeah, it's real painful. She's beautiful, and yeah [he sighs deeply and continues], it's frustrating to me to look at someone as pretty as her and say that there's no way I can get back into this relationship with her because of things in the past." He tells Chris how difficult this process has been for him, expressing sadness for the loss of such a beautiful image of an ideal woman. She is so attractive to him and yet he is unable to be with her; he is drawn to her (seemingly superficial qualities) and at the same time he has a strong conviction about their unsuitability as a couple. There is a push-and-pull here, one that seems to be explained by the contrast in how Helene appeared on the series and how she is on the special.

On *The Bachelor*, Helene repeatedly claimed to eschew drama. In fact, she threatens to leave the show on the second episode if the drama does not die down in the women's house. Aaron commiserates, saying he is also having a hard time with all the drama, but he asks her to stay. Helene stands out from the other women not only because of her distress over the drama the other women are causing but also because she is characterized (as the host mentions in the special) as a challenge for Aaron. The series shows that only by episode six does Aaron feel confident of Helene's feelings for him, while he knows much earlier how the other women feel about him. Helene is seen acting as if she, not Aaron, is the prize to be won.

The series never shows Helene crying. On the special "Aaron and Helene Tell All," however, this woman who had been the image of composure and restraint on *The Bachelor* loses her composure in the very first minutes of the interview and is on the brink of tears or in tears throughout the remainder of it. This Helene is devastated, incapable of containing her emotions, unable, it would seem, to say one full sentence about Aaron without her eyes welling up with tears. This is not the same Helene who eschewed drama and presented a challenge to Aaron. The intriguing enigma that is Helene on *The Bachelor* is transgressed by the devastated, emotional Helene on the special. Helene's mystique has unraveled right before our eyes. She is an emotional mess. This is hardly the woman who won the bachelor's heart. This version of Helene, we are meant to infer, is the woman who lost his heart (the special makes it clear he is the one who broke things off).

How did Helene change from an attractive and enigmatic woman to one who is devastated, emotional, unable to contain her emotions? Why does Aaron, almost sadly and wistfully, keep drawing our attention to Helene's beauty, as if something precious has been ruined? Why are the two images of Helene in such stark contrast? This transformation from an originally appealing and desirable woman (to the bachelor, and potentially to viewers) into a woman unable to contain her emotions, and therefore unappealing, is a recurring trope in the BI. Many women suffer this fate.

Consistency is important. Nothing new should be revealed by a woman; rather, something already known should be confirmed. This is Helene's fatal flaw. Deanna Pappas, for instance, star of season four of *The Bachelorette*, cries at almost every rose ceremony, so overcome is she by her feelings for the men and the momentousness of the decisions she needs to make. Her crying confirms what we have already seen of her: that she takes the process seriously and that she has strong feelings for the men. Trista, star of the first season of *The Bachelorette*, also cries and displays emotion often, but always in ways that are consistent with how the series shows her wanting to present herself and always in line with the image the series has already constructed of her. For example, she is in tears on the first episode of *The Bachelorette* after handing out the roses at the rose ceremony because she feels bad about eliminating the men. As with Deanna, this adds to her existing characterization as compassionate, confirming that she does not take her task lightly. In another scene, her eyes well up with tears when Ryan, the man she eventually chooses, reads her one of his poems, confirming to us that she has strong feelings for him. Trista's crying in these instances, like Deanna's, verifies what we have already come to expect of her, namely, that she is a caring woman who has deep feelings. These images of Trista as emotional support and maintain how she is presented throughout the season. Importantly, her emotionality does not distract her from her purpose, finding love.

Displays of emotion do not necessarily reveal something unattractive about a woman. However, there are particular ways in which a woman's display of emotion can be framed as dangerous. The danger is twofold: for the other people, because the woman is unstable and there is no way of knowing what she might do next, and for the woman, because these displays signal her imminent departure from the series and concomitantly her unsuitability for love.

This chapter looks at moments when, through a focus on emotional displays, the BI reveals something a woman is shown explicitly not wanting revealed, when the emotional display exposes the woman, revealing her to be quite different from how she was originally presented. This revelation verifies a woman as undesirable and violates her intended (as the series constructs it) presentation of self. This process is particularly important for critical feminist scholars, because the aspects that ultimately work to unravel the women are also intricately connected to conventional feminine requirements for emotional behavior (here pushed to seeming extremes).

The Money Shot

I use the term "money shot" to describe displays of emotion by women in the BI that are presented as excessive and frightening. Scholars studying film pornography use the term "money shot" to characterize the culminating moment in a pornographic film where the ejaculating penis occupies center stage. Feminist scholars examine the implications of this shot in centering male desire and eliding female desire (McClintock, 1993; Williams, 1993). Television scholar Grindstaff (2002) uses the term to describe the climactic moment on daytime talk shows when guests reveal their secrets in an emotional manner. I build on these uses of the term to examine the implications of the display of women's emotions as the climactic moment in the BI shows. The "money shot" is the spectacular revelation of a woman's emotions, signaling that the woman is unable to control herself and unfit for love and inspiring viewer pleasure in her failure to find love. A woman who provides the "money shot" in the BI loses her appeal as an object of a man's desire. While this way of showing women's emotions is apparent in popular media and in other reality shows, the BI is a particularly good place to examine this way of showing women's emotions since it centers on romantic relationships, with an explicit emphasis on feelings and emotions.

The Bachelor uses the "money shot" for key moments over several episodes, layering these to build an image of a woman unfit for love. At least one woman in every season provides "money shots" (some more poignant than others) and is therefore characterized as an unsuitable romantic partner for the bachelor and as threatening to his well-being. This woman becomes the center of the narrative for several episodes, the star of the series, until her elimination. To provide a detailed analysis of how the "money shot" operates, I examine how the series characterizes two women from *The Bachelor*, Christi from season two and Lee-Ann from season four, though this trope of the "money shot" is not limited to these women and is used in almost every season to characterize one woman.

Some theory on the "money shot" helps outline how this mechanism operates in the BI. Grindstaff (2002) insists that the raison d'être of the talk show is to elicit a "money shot" from guests, which she describes as a shot in which:

> joy, sorrow, rage, or remorse [are] expressed in visible, bodily terms. It is the moment when tears well up in a woman's eyes and her voice catches in sadness and pain as she describes having lost her child to a preventable disease; when a man tells his girlfriend that he's been sleeping with another woman and her jaw drops in rage and disbelief . . . These moments have become the hallmark of the genre, central to its claim to authenticity as well as to its negative reputation. According to producers, the more emotional and volatile the guests and audience members, the more real (and the more "ordinary") they are. (pp. 19-20)

The "money shot" is the display of intense emotion, and it is the climactic moment in the talk show. The shot verifies the authenticity of the moment. It is proof that guests have felt real emotion. Grindstaff (2002) distinguishes between a "soft-core" and a "hard-core" "money shot." The "soft-core" "money shot" is confessional, used for middle-class white women. This type of shot is "feminine" and "based on heartache or joy rather than conflict and anger" (the basis for the "hard-core" "money shot") (pp. 26-27). The "soft-core" "money shot" applies to my discussion:

> like the orgasmic cum shot of pornographic films, the money shot of talk shows makes visible the precise moment of letting go, of losing control, of surrendering to the body and its "animal" emotions. It is the loss of the "civilized" self that occurs when the body transcends social and cultural control, revealing human behavior in its "raw" rather than its "cooked form." (p. 20)

Grindstaff does not discuss the consequences of this loss, except to specify that it is at the center of the drama of the talk show and that different types of "money shots" are used to mark class. The "money shot" in the BI often includes a loss of control of the body—sobbing, for instance—but the key loss is over the presentation of self. As well, while the loss of control is the dramatic center of the series, it has grave consequences for the participant who provides the shot, since it signifies a transgression of her original image and of how she wants to present herself (loss of the "civilized" self Grindstaff refers to). The "money shot" reveals women as undesirable romantic partners for the bachelor because they cannot control or contain their emotions. Consequently, unlike in the talk show, in the BI the "money shot" always puts women at risk.

Phallic Economy

Grindstaff's use of the term "money shot" does not take into account either the phallic economy of mainstream heterosexual pornography from which the term stems or the merging of emotional displays and pornographic style, both of which are important in understanding the purpose of the shot for my analysis. In film pornography, the "money shot" is provided only by the male body. It is the "cum-shot . . . called in the industry the 'money shot', because men are paid more for the shot, and consumers get their 'money's worth'" (McClintock, 1993, p. 124). The shot is "devoted to revealing visible evidence of phallic power and potency" (Williams, 1993, p. 244). However, many of the bodies Grindstaff (2002) describes as "letting go," "losing control," "surrendering to the body and its 'animal' emotions" (p. 20) are female, and all the bodies that provide the "money shot" in the BI are female.

In film pornography, women's bodies and the exploration of their inner sanctums are visually central until the "money shot." Only in the climactic moment of the "money shot" does the penis take center stage (McClintock, 1993, p. 123; Williams, 1993, p. 242), and even then a female body is almost always the backdrop for the shot or the surface upon which it occurs (face, breasts, and so forth). Women's bodies are an essential part of the mechanism that produces the "money shot": the shot is elicited and aroused through female bodies. In this sense, using the term "money shot" to describe how the BI uses the display of emotional women situates the entire process within a phallic economy in which male power and female disempowerment are central. The "money shot" in the BI shows a female participant's loss of control, an emotional display written on the body but not limited to the body that signifies a loss of mastery of the self. In the BI, it represents a transgression in which the display, the exposure of a woman's inner, private, emotional self, puts her at a disadvantage and promotes, supports, and bolsters male privilege. The term "money shot" locates the display of female emotions as pornographic, that is, as an explicit, sensational depiction with the intention to arouse the viewer (in this instance not to arouse sexual desire, but to provide some kind of pleasure through the arousal of disgust and fear).

Once the "money shot" is given in the BI, a woman becomes "damaged goods." This is not the case in the talk show, where a woman providing the money shot is the center of an episode but the shot does not necessarily mark her negatively thereafter. This difference in the narrative purpose of the "money shot" may be due to the difference in format. An episode of a talk show contains an entire storyline, while an episode of *The Bachelor* is only part of a larger storyline. In *The Bachelor*, the "money shot" comes near the middle of a storyline about a woman who fails at love and is followed by one or two episodes during which the story of her downfall is told. After a woman provides her first "money shot," the BI shows her spiraling out of control. By the time she is eliminated, the audience has anticipated her elimination. The "money shot" propels the story of how a woman fails at love. This setup constructs the bachelor as a dupe for tolerating the woman's overemotional behavior for so long but also ensures our sympathies are with him when he does eliminate her. The bachelor generously invites the woman to stay despite her behavior. She adds insult to injury by not rectifying her behavior when given a second chance, therefore overstaying her welcome. In contrast, the "money shot" is not only the center of the storyline of the talk show (which unfolds in a single episode), it *is* the story.

Melodrama

In her essay theorizing women's emotionality on television, Joyrich (1992) suggests that melodrama is so pervasive on television that it is hard to distinguish as a separate genre (p. 229). The BI shows share more than a few characteristics with the genre of melodrama. While I do not wish to lodge my argument within a genre studies framework, I want to list features of the BI that fit the category of melodrama to situate it as part of a feminine genre that explores the emotions of women and that is geared to a female audience.

Aspects Joyrich (1992) lists as characteristic of melodrama highlight how much the BI shows share with the genre, especially *The Bachelor* series (where the focus is on women): (1) music often orchestrates emotion (p. 229): the carousel scene discussed below is a good example; (2) the rhythm of the series follows the emotional experiences of participants (p. 229): the narrative in *The Bachelor* centers around participants' emotional displays; (3) melodrama makes good use of close-ups (p. 234): the BI relies on close-ups of women's tearful and emotional faces; (4) intimate gestures are central (p. 234): caressing, kissing, and hugging are among the main activities of participants; (5) much of the action centers on the dichotomy between good and bad (p. 231): in *The Bachelor*, the "good" women vs. "bad" women dynamic is fundamental; (6) social turmoil is placed in private, emotional terms (p. 229): gender inequalities are expressed through women's emotional response to issues that arise in personal interactions with other participants; (7) female subjectivity is privileged (p. 240): though the men hold more power than the women in *The Bachelor* (to eliminate women from the series), the story is all about the women and their (supposed) perspective; and (8) the appeal is to a female audience (p. 240): the subject matter of the BI shows—finding a romantic partner—indicates the target audience is women.

The formal elements of melodrama are also important in how the BI conveys "realness" of emotion. Joyrich (1992) specifies that melodrama

> allows us both closeness and certainty through its appeal to a prelinguistic system of gesture and tableau that aims beyond language to immediate understanding. In its attempt to render meaning visible and recapture the ineffable, melodrama emphasizes gestures, postures, frozen moments and expressions. Television strengthens these conventions as it clearly directs attention to the revelations of facial expression, providing close-ups that disclose what before only a lover or a mother ever saw. TV melodrama, like its precursors in the theatre and cinema, thus tends to deny the complex processes of signification and to collapse representation onto the real, assuring its audience of firm stakes of meaning. (p. 245)

Not only does melodrama focus on the personal and the emotional, this is formalistically emphasized by visually capturing it on film. Melodrama conveys "reality" through the representation of visual cues that signal emotion has been felt. Further, proof of this emotion is written on the body in ways that can be visually read through images captured by the camera.

Visual Knowledge

Melodrama shares with the genres of film pornography and reality television the desire to show real intimate emotions written on the body, seeking to present the real as lived by real people. While the BI shows share with melodrama the impetus to put emotions on display, especially typically feminine ones (connected to love and relationships), film pornography explores only sexual emotions. However, reality television and film pornography are both caught up in what Williams (1989) calls the "frenzy of the visible" (p. 194), that is, the desire to show and to visibly inscribe onto the body intense bodily responses. Williams (1989, 1993) emphasizes the importance of the visibility of real sexual acts in pornography in verifying that pleasure, intense feeling, has been felt. I quote her at length because she is helpful in explaining the importance of providing visual knowledge of emotions in the BI:

> In this first crisis—the crisis of the visibility of pleasure in a genre committed to showing the spectacle of "it"—pornography seeks, through the deployment of what Foucault calls the 'scientia sexualis,' to confess the irrefutable, self-evident truths of sex. One goal of film and visual pornography thus coincides precisely with the intensifying goal of modern Western society's quest for the knowledge of pleasure, and thus one pole of hard-core heterosexual pornography is perhaps best characterized as a regime of the visual knowledge of pleasure. This aspect of the genre is characterized by a cinéma vérité devotion to the revelation-confession of real bodies caught in the act of sexual plea-

sure—in, for example, the "meat shot." Here, in confirming close-up, is irrefutable, visible evidence of penetration, really taking place, with no possible faking. Here, also, is a primary heterosexual reproductive "norm" of sexuality. (1993, p. 241)

As explored in Chapter 1, part of the mechanism that verifies the authenticity of participants in the BI is that they are shown to be their real selves despite being under surveillance. Paradoxically, then, behaving authentically in a constructed and contrived setting, under surveillance, works to verify authenticity of the self. This mirrors part of what happens in film pornography.[1] In film pornography, actors are employed, not real people as in reality television, yet the acts the porn actors perform are real (penetration occurs). The "cinéma vérité" style, as Williams calls it, suggests that the display on film is of people experiencing real things. This is the parallel between film pornography and the BI: they share a desire to display real things occurring between people and to present this in visual terms. In film pornography, the aim is to show the human body experiencing pleasure, and in the BI the quest is to display people experiencing real emotions.

In the BI, as in melodrama, the quest is to expose the emotional inner sanctums of female subjectivity: the female body experiencing emotion—a pornography of emotion. Integral to this quest is a desire to show real emotion as experienced by real people. For example, in the mise-en-scène of a scene I describe shortly, the series revels in Christi's emotionality: the camera moves closer as she becomes more emotional, and the audio reveals the extent of her sobbing. It is a sensational and lurid portrayal of Christi's emotions that thrives on the "frenzy of the visible" (Williams, 1989, p. 194).

Film pornography and the BI deploy what Williams (1983) calls a "scientia" (borrowing from Foucault, as quoted above) for producing "visual knowledge"—in pornography, visual knowledge of pleasure, in the BI, visual knowledge of emotion. In each, visual evidence of a sense of the uncontrolled is provided; though the result is elicited and produced, it is nonetheless physiological (crying, anger, having an orgasm) and beyond human control—irrefutable bodily signs of pleasure or emotion. However, while crying, for example, suggests emotion, it does not necessarily mean the emotion is connected to the act represented (some can cry at will, or participants may be crying or angry about something other than what the narrative leads us to believe). Analogously, while the cinematic image of penetration in pornography provides irrefutable evidence that intercourse has taken place, it cannot prove that pleasure has been felt, nor can visual signs of male ejaculation provide positive proof of pleasure (even men can "fake it"), only proof of a physiological response (that may be decontextualized through the editing process). The image is always marked with the editing and production process. Nonetheless, what is constructed in film pornography and in the BI is a sense of having revealed an inner, private, previously hidden self—a naked self (literally in one instance). In each case we are given visual "proof" of a moment in which someone has become unable to control his/herself, when bodily desires and drives overtake rational mental control.[2]

Christi's First Money Shot

Christi from season two of *The Bachelor* and Lee-Ann from season four are two extreme and complex examples of "grotesque" and "unruly" women initially cast as desirable romantic partners. Like beautifully wrapped packages that raise our expectations for what lies inside, Christi and Lee-Ann's attractive exteriors fill the bachelors with anticipation, only quickly to be unraveled by the BI to reveal an inside that disappoints and, at times, frighten.

In response to the host's question, on the first episode of season two of *The Bachelor*, about which girl really caught his attention, bachelor Aaron immediately says "Christi." However, this good first impression is marred over the next three episodes. As the host tells us in the season's "The Women Tell All" episode, "this show is full of memorable moments, and Christi provided a lot of them." Christi supplies one such memorable moment on the second episode with her first "money-shot." At the beginning of a group date with five women, Aaron seems content to receive Christi's affection, their arms wrapped around each other as they talk intimately. However, halfway through the date, something appears to be amiss with Christi. Viewers see Christi sitting at a dinner table with some of the other women talking to Anindita about Christi's dislike of a third participant, Suzanne (who is not present, nor is the bachelor). Next viewers see Christi run off in tears as Anindita tries to explain that she is not trying to attack her. Angela, another woman on the date, runs after Christi. Then a medium shot of Christi standing in the corner of a room crying, with Angela standing in front of her, back to the camera. Christi sobs and is barely able to speak. The camera moves in for a close-up as Christi says, pointing to her heart, "I'm sensitive." She sobs loudly, her head moving up and down. Angela comforts her by murmuring that she understands. Christi puts her head in her hands, her sobs mounting as the camera zooms in for a closer shot of her crying. Christi looks up from her hands at Angela and continues to cry, still pointing to her heart, while exclaiming between sobs that she is hurt by what people say about her. Angela tries to reassure her, telling her it was only one person who was saying things. Christi interjects, tearfully repeating that what was said hurt her feelings, telling Angela that her heart hurts. Christi continues to sob. Angela again reminds Christi that it was only one person who was saying things. Christi sobs some more. Angela works to calm Christi by telling her not to get so upset, instructing her to breathe deeply. The camera zooms out to a long shot as Christi asserts, this time barely audibly because of her sobs, that all she wants is to go home. Angela interjects that she's positive Christi doesn't really want to go home, reminding Christi of her good feelings about the bachelor, imploring her not to let one person destroy this opportunity for her.

The actual content of the exchange between Angela and Christi is inconsequential to the overall narrative of the series, but the visual display of Christi's emotionality is absolutely central in situating her as excessively emotional, unable to control herself, and a disruptive presence. This is the first of several "money shots" Christi provides, and she never regains her original allure. What marks this as a "money shot" is Christi's inability to contain her emotions. Sobs wrack her body and she is barely able to speak. She seems not in control of her feelings, blurting out that she wants to give up on the entire process despite earlier scenes where she attests to her strong desire to remain on the show. The suggestion is that her emotions are so strong they make her behave in ways she might not otherwise. Christi's emotional outburst reveals a new side to her, an unsettling side different from the alluring woman to whom viewers were originally introduced. Indeed, the attractive woman who "knocked the socks off" the bachelor at the outset has quickly transformed into a tearful, emotional mess right before our eyes.

"That" Girl

Christi's image is shot through and through with her failure to contain herself, made all the more poignant by her expressed desire to do so. For example, in a scene at the end of the fateful date when she provides her first "money shot," viewers see Christi and Aaron go outside as she says to him, in tears, "I was having such a great time. . . and I just don't want to be *that* girl . . . I'm not that girl." In the next shot, of Christi and Aaron hugging, Aaron recounts in voice-over that they hugged for a long time. He says repeatedly that Christi would just not let go of him, that she was holding on and holding on to him. The scene then cuts to a shot of Christi whispering to Aaron how rare it is for her to feel this way about a guy and confessing that she thinks he is incredible. They hug some more, and then they kiss. While this scene plays out, Aaron says in voice-over that he thought Christi felt a lot better after they kissed. This scene is followed by a shot of Aaron saying to the camera, "It eased the tension and made everything much more comfortable for everyone." The next shot is of Christi tearfully telling the camera, "Yeah, I love Aaron. I love that when he was holding me I couldn't catch my breath. I don't know. I'm reeling, and I'm scared." The following shot is of Christi and Aaron still hugging. Later on in the episode, Aaron tells the camera that he was surprised by how emotional Christi became in Napa Valley.

The series suggests in this scene that Aaron is simply trying to comfort Christi but her feelings are so overwhelming that she has grown unreasonably attached to him—she just cannot let go! Viewers are then given proof that this is indeed the case (and not just Aaron's perspective) when Christi tearfully confesses to the camera that she loves Aaron so much she is frightened and cannot breathe. Her emotional responses are presented as beyond her control and inscribed on her body (her eyes are teary, she is having trouble breathing).

Part of Christi's construction as out-of-control relies on her awareness that her behavior is causing problems. Her comment about not being *"that girl"* implies she is conscious that she needs to control her behavior lest she become *"that* girl." Yet the images of her continuing to behave in the same manner after making this statement suggest her behavior, her emotional responses, are unwitting, that they happen despite her desire and her attempts to be otherwise, despite her best intentions.

The series persists in showing Christi unable to stop her excessively emotional behavior regardless of her expressed desire to do so: this behavior characterizes her. Right before the rose ceremony at the end of the second episode, Christi says to Aaron that she is really sorry she made the date "emotionally charged." For a short time, this apology seems to work; Aaron offers Christi a rose at the ceremony. He tells the host he kept Christi because of how impressed he was with her when they first met, saying he wants to give her another chance. In other words, despite the fact that Christi has transgressed Aaron's first impression of her (and her own sense of herself), the bachelor is willing to give her another chance to prove she really is the attractive woman he originally thought she was. However, in the very last scene of this episode, as the credits roll, viewers see Christi, in a medium shot that slowly moves into a close-up of her face, saying to another woman, "I've never had anyone sweep me off my feet like Aaron has. I can love Aaron. Like I could fall in love hard. I think I love him now. I think he's a great guy. I love him." Her intense feelings spill out, and this is the impression of Christi the audience is left with for that week. On the next episode, in Christi's last plea in her video message right before she is eliminated (a short video message given to the bachelor before the rose ceremony), she is presented as all too aware of her transgression. She says: "I'm sorry for all the drama. If you trust in what we felt the first night and give me a chance, I think we could be great." Here Christi tries to reclaim the image of herself from the first night (when she was still an attractive prospect for Aaron), asking Aaron to forget about the emotional self she displayed after.

Disrobing a Fatal Attraction

The importance of the "money shot" is that it signals Christi is out of control. Christi's behavior before the first "money shot" suggests she never intended to show this emotional, out-of-control side of herself. It crept out unwittingly, revealing who she "really" is. Here the interplay between surveillance and authenticity is crucial in verifying the realness of her emotions. So strong and real were her emotions that not even the presence of cameras and her strong desire to im-press the bachelor can stop them from spilling out, ultimately betraying her expressed intention to not be "that" girl.

The tension between who Christi says she wants to be and who the series reveals her to be is troubling. Add to this the visual proof of Christi's inability to control herself, and the unraveling of Christi becomes an invasive, aggressive action by the series, performed against her will (she is shown not wanting this side to come out). The revealing of this real, inner self works to justify and provide a rationale for Christi's elimination. As well, this revealing situates the bachelor's elimination of Christi as a heroic act, since it restores order by removing an unpredictable and potentially dangerous element from the show. However, what exactly is the threat Christi poses? From what has the bachelor protected himself and his harem?

On the third episode, Aaron tells the camera that he thinks Christi "kinda had a fatal attraction thing going on" (a term borrowed from the 1987 film *Fatal Attraction*, discussed shortly). "She was telling the girls that she was in love with me. She was very emotional in Napa Valley, and I don't know why." In the next shot, eerie carnival music plays loudly (suggesting something is not right), and viewers see a long shot of Aaron and Christi looking oversized sitting on colorful animal figures on a carousel, the creatures moving up and down as the carousel turns round and round. The camera focuses on Christi in close-up as she says to Aaron that she feels like she "got off on the wrong impression with the whole date" (referring to the date where she provides her first "money-shot"). Then a close-up of Aaron slumped over his animal as it moves up and down, not saying anything and looking very uncomfortable. Cut to a close-up of Christi saying she thought Anindita, the woman who confronted her, was trying to stir up trouble by implying Christi was an awful person. Again, viewers see a close-up shot of Aaron looking very uncomfortable. Christi continues, telling Aaron she isn't the kind of person to cause trouble and doesn't ever want others to think she doesn't like them. She continues to insist that she wants people to feel comfortable around her, to have a good time when she's around. Christi talks about how much it bothered her to think someone had a problem with her. She says, finally, "I'm not, like, I'm not an emotional freak!" He responds with "Yeah," still appearing terribly uncomfortable. The next shot is of Christi looking anxiously at Aaron.

Though Christi says she wants everyone to feel comfortable around her, the shots of Aaron's tense face and his monosyllabic answers suggest he is decidedly uncomfortable in her presence. The mise-en-scène, with the eerie carnival music and the absurd-looking animals moving up and down and round and round, implies that this is not a comfortable environment and that there might be danger lurking just beneath the surface, about to burst forth (the music and carnival atmosphere are suggestive of a "jack-in-the-box" kind of tension where there is a hyperawareness that something frightening is about to happen, but it is unclear exactly when it will occur; danger is imminent). In the next scene, viewers get confirmation from Christi herself that something is amiss. Christi says to the camera, "What happened? What did I say? What did I do? I mean on the last date, I mean, obviously, he and I kissed. We were holding hands. Today there was none of that, none." Once again, the series portrays Christi as quite aware of her predicament, aware of the discomfort she has caused, clearly wishing she could change the situation, wishing she was not seen as "an emotional freak."

There is a cruel irony to the situation. The more Christi speaks about what is going on, the more she confesses her feelings (one of the consistent behavior requirements for participants on the series), the worse she appears. Yet speaking about what is occurring seems the only way to show she is not, in Aaron's words, a girl with a "fatal attraction." Nonetheless, the label sticks throughout the season. Christi mentions it in "The Women Tell All" episode (denying she is this kind of woman), and Aaron uses it on the eighth episode (long after Christi is eliminated) to describe Christi to his father.

Even Christi's attempts to remedy the situation are cast as excessive, re-confirming that she really is out-of-control. For instance, continuing the conversation on the carousel cited above, Christi says to Aaron, "I knew that I had to talk to you about what had happened, and I really would have rather just, like, been able to forget all about it . . . I think it still bothers you." He tells her it does bother him a little. She laments that things have completely changed between them, at which point Aaron interjects with "yeah" and she continues, "I just think things are weird now. I just feel weird now." Christi tells some of the other women after this exchange that her alone time with Aaron "just sucked," explaining that "Part of it was just, I was so caught off guard by him bringing all of it up again. I mean, I thought we were, you know, I'm totally over what happened. I mean, we talked about it several times, and I just don't know what to say."

At the end of this episode (three), Christi is eliminated. Not only does the series show Aaron no longer interested in Christi, it constructs her dismissal as necessary because she poses a potential threat to him. After eliminating Christi, Aaron says, "A girl like Christi, who's been very emotional, that's a concern for me, that she's been able to fall that head over heels for me in such a short amount of time. She's very emotionally unstable, if you will. That bothers me. I don't know how to deal with it. I really don't." The implication is that Aaron should not have to deal with this, that this is not Aaron's problem but Christi's. Since the bachelor is the protagonist, with whom our sympathies are meant to lie, he is cast as the victim of Christi's inability to control her emotions, with the suggestion that he may become a bigger victim to Christi's "fatal attraction" and emotional instability if he does not get rid of her immediately (fool me once, shame on you, fool me twice . . .).

The "fatal attraction" label sheds some insight into the danger posed by women like Christi who provide the "money shot," women who are unable to control their emotions, who grow attached too quickly to men, who make victims out of "good" men. Christi's construction as the "fatal attraction" girl relies on her initial characterization by the series as a very attractive and appealing young woman, an ideal creature of femininity—like Alex Forrest, the woman played by Glenn Close who has a "fatal attraction" in the film of the same title. The bachelor is drawn to Christi the first time he sees her, just as Dan Gallagher (Michael Douglas) in the film is drawn to Close's character. Aaron is soon repulsed, however, by Christi's neediness, emotionality, and affection, as is Douglas's character by the same traits in Close's character. The women's initial attractiveness to the men seems to mark their later behaviors as particularly repugnant—repugnant because such alluring and attractive women have become so unattractive to them. However, the women are not simply unattractive and repugnant, they pose a threat to the men. They are dangerous because they are ruled by their emotions and their intense feelings for the men, and because they can be so enticing.

By using the label "fatal attraction" to characterize Christi's feelings for him, Aaron positions himself as the victim of a woman who is unstable, not in control of herself and potentially harmful to him. Close's character, for example, kidnaps Douglas' character's daughter and tries to kill his wife. So who knows what Christi might do if Aaron does not get rid of her immediately? The "fatal attraction" label ultimately renders Christi dispensable, and, more importantly, implies she must be eliminated to protect the bachelor and the other women in the harem.

What if?

Since BI shows are constructed through the editing and production process involved in putting together a TV show, the use of the "money shot" by the creators is strategic, meant to produce a specific result. It is worth considering alternate stories that might have been told about Christi, stories where the "money shot" would not characterize Christi as unstable and dangerous, or stories where the "money shot" would have been unnecessary. Doing this helps pinpoint the specific ways that the BI constructs the story it tells about Christi.

For instance, how does the emphasis on Christi incessantly trying to explain her actions characterize her? Though the series does not show Aaron asking Christi to explain herself, it is worth pausing to consider the possibility that this is what happened, as it would suggest an alternate narrative. In this new narrative, it is Aaron who requests constant confessions, talk about feelings and emotions from Christi, and not Christi who willingly—though sometimes unwittingly—provides these. This "what if" scenario would explain why Christi keeps saying things like "I'm not an emotional freak." Perhaps it is Aaron who requires Christi to speak about what has happened, as she expresses when she says she does not understand why he keeps bringing it up when she's over the whole thing. If so, then maybe Christi is emotional about always having to explain her actions, distressed that none of her explanations seem sufficient.

As well, it is worth asking what would happen to the story about Christi if the emotional scenes, and Aaron's comments about them, were removed. How does the series' foregrounding of Christi's emotionality shape the story about Christi and Aaron? Without this foregrounding, we would be left with Aaron and Christi professing their mutual affection for and attraction to one another, images of the couple being affectionate and enjoying each other's company, scenes of Christi telling the camera how much she likes Aaron, seemingly confirming that the two are falling for one another (rather than marking Christi as overemotional). Perhaps there might also have been shots of Aaron professing his affection for Christi (surely in the footage there were scenes of Aaron declaring his affection for Christi). In other words, a very different story might have been told about Christi.

Lee-Ann

The second woman examined in this chapter is Lee-Ann from season four of *The Bachelor*. While she too is unraveled to reveal an emotional and unattractive woman, unlike Christi she expresses anger and indignation at her predicament and in the end lodges a bit of a critique at the BI. Bachelor Bob is very much taken with Lee-Ann from the outset, just as Aaron is taken with Christi in the beginning. On the first episode, when Bob tells the host which women really caught his attention, he begins with Lee-Ann, describing her as "beautiful," "naturally pretty," "comfortable with herself." On the second episode, Bob tells the camera that Lee-Ann has a "beautiful girl-next-door quality" and that they have a lot of chemistry together. Unfortunately, Lee-Ann's charms fade over the first five episodes as she is seen fighting with the women in the house and professing to the camera, the bachelor, and the other women that she does not care what anyone thinks of her. Viewers eventually see her breaking down tearfully to the bachelor and the other women because, in the end, she does care what they think of her.

Unlike with Christi, the focus is primarily on Lee-Ann's conflicts with the other women, not on problems with her interactions with the bachelor. In fact, her relationship with Bob appears to be going well when he eliminates her, and he does not provide an explanation for her elimination. The images of Lee-Ann that we are left with are of her alternately being arrogantly self-assured and arguing with the other women, and breaking down tearfully, sobbing to the bachelor and to the women about how upset she is that none of the women like her. In the absence of any explanation from Bob, the construction of Lee-Ann as emotionally transgressing her own assertions about who she is provide the most tangible answer to why she is eliminated. She is not in control of herself and as such is dangerous to the bachelor and the other women, and, most importantly, she is unfit for love.

On the fourth episode, right before the rose ceremony, Lee-Ann provides the first of her "money shots." While Bob and Lee-Ann are talking in private, he comments that she looks upset. After some prodding from him, she tells him she is miserable. Shown in close-up, she says she was having a great time until the group date, when nobody would talk to her. As she speaks, her eyes well up with tears and her voice begins to quiver. Still in close-up, she tries to speak, but all that comes out is "and..." and her voice trails off as she closes her mouth, unable to complete the sentence, so overcome is she with emotion. This is followed by a close-up of Bob as he reassures her that he likes talking to her. He suggests they go for a walk before returning to the house. The camera moves into a close-up of Lee-Ann's face as she says, with a smile, "yeah," her voice quivering and her eyes full of tears.

The next series of shots go from medium to long to slightly overhead long shots of the couple standing in a darkened corner of the garden talking. Viewers never see Bob and Lee-Ann's faces clearly, only their bodies and hand motions. We hear Lee-Ann whisper, voice still quivering and full of emotion, sounding like she is crying, "this sucks. For me, you have no idea. I've never been the source of controversy in my life." Voice full of emotion, Lee-Ann talks more about how hard this situation has been for her, lamenting that falling for someone should not be this hard. In a medium shot from the side of the couple, Lee-Ann tells the bachelor that though she is there for the right reasons, she did not sign up for all this other stuff. Bob tries to reassure her by telling her how much he enjoys his time with her. As she begins to respond, viewers see a medium shot of the couple standing in the dark, Lee-Ann wiping tears away from her face and telling Bob she has strong feelings for him but doesn't know where she stands with him. She adds that sometimes she just wants to leave. He says she should know where she stands. She states, finally, that unless she's going to be one of the final women, he should send her home. He responds, "duly noted."

Lee-Ann's first "money shot" is more subdued than Christi's. What is similar is the loss of control in the display of emotion. The series shows Lee-Ann trying unsuccessfully to control her emotions: she stops herself from speaking so she can control her emotions; she puts on a smile though her eyes are full of tears.

After the couple enters the garden in the scene above, viewers are put in the position of voyeur through the use of surveillance-style camera work. This style is rarely used in the BI[3] and marks the scene as unique, making it stand out and alerting viewers to the fact that what we are seeing is important. The scene is dark, and it is impossible to see Bob and Lee-Ann's facial expressions. The perspective is as if the viewer is hiding behind the bushes, surveilling the couple in their "natural habitat." This suggests that what is shown is real, because it is being expressed in an environment in which the participants are "unaware" that they are being surveilled (of course they are aware and they are still wearing their microphones, since we hear them clearly). Narratively, this moment is framed as a private one. Bob suggests to Lee-Ann that they go for a walk just as she begins to cry, implying he wants to give her some privacy during an emotional time. The cinematography reinforces that what we see is private, because we seem to be watching covertly as the action unfolds in a darkened corner of the garden, making it difficult for us to see much of the action.

The first "money shot" shows Lee-Ann revealing a side of herself that is different from her original presentation of self, signaling her loss of control over her presentation of self. Here she is quite different from the very self-confident woman we are introduced to originally. On the first episode, she says to the camera, "I think that I'm smart. I think I'm witty and cute. I think I have a good head on my shoulders. I'm well-rounded, I'm down to earth and I think I have a shot at getting a ring at the end of this." By episode three, however, most of the women in the house actively dislike Lee-Ann (they vote her least compatible with Bob).[4] In trying to explain how she feels about the situation in a heated exchange with one of the other women, Lee-Ann continues to assert her self-confidence and self-knowledge, playing out perfectly what I term in Chapter 5 "the therapeutics of the self" (affirmation of pride in who one is and in one's ability to be consistent in one's behavior): "I know who I am, and that's fine with me. So it doesn't matter what you think of me, or what anyone thinks of me. I'm fine with myself, and I'm confident with where I stand with Bob." Lee-Ann is presented as not caring what the other women think of her, which she expresses on the fourth episode when she says that she is sure "some of the girls were jealous. Does it look like I care? Did you see me cry when we run into each other? Hell no! I am not here to be the bridesmaid in their wedding. I am here to be with Bob." However, at this point the series casts some doubt about Lee-Anne's self-confidence. The next overhead shot, which turns into a long shot, is of Lee-Ann dressed up for her date (in a ball gown), sitting alone in the middle of a huge living room waiting for Bob. The shot emphasizes the big room with Lee-Ann all alone, visually illustrating her alienation in the house.

As the scene of the "money shot" described above illustrates, viewers discover that Lee-Ann does actually care what others think of her, that she will in fact cry. Unlike Trish from season five of The Bachelor, discussed in the next chapter, Lee-Ann is unable to maintain her stance of not caring what others think of her. Indeed, Trish is remarkable because she is so disliked by everyone and yet she emerges as a strong and consistent character: she is never unraveled, revealed to be someone she did not appear to be at first. It is clear from the outset who Trish is. In fact, the host warns viewers on the first episode that Trish will be the most despised woman in bachelor history. Although Trish has different values and opinions (about marriage, children, sex, money) than the other women (and these do not mesh well with those upheld by the BI), she is consistent in showing these throughout her time on the series. None of what the bachelor discovers about Trish contradicts what he (or viewers) originally see of Trish; it only confirms what has already been revealed. This is very different from Lee-Ann's predicament. Lee-Ann is not only inconsistent in her behavior, she surprises by revealing an insecure and emotional side of herself. As with Christi and Helene, it is the contrast between how she originally appears and who she turns into that is the problem.

Lee-Ann's most powerful "money shot" comes on episode five, the episode after her first "money shot." Viewers see a long shot of Lee-Ann alone, sitting on a swinging bench in the garden. She then gets up, goes into the house and rounds up the women. We watch as she tearfully tells the women that she realizes she pulled away from the group, that she may have given them the impression she did not want to be friends or did not like them. She begins to sob as she apologizes, telling the women she would do anything to make things up to them. She tearfully says that she feels alone in the house, that this has been very difficult for her, and that she fears being eliminated. Then she adds "and you all know I never cry. Cuz I just, cuz this is just not me. And I hate being the one that doesn't fit in, and I'm really sorry that I pulled away from you all, and if there's anything I could do to fix the situation then I would."

Close-up shots of Meredith (who becomes the star of the second season of *The Bachelorette*) looking horrified intersperse the scene, and at one point the scene cuts to a shot of Meredith saying to the camera (in a different setting) that she is fed up with all the drama Lee-Ann is constantly causing. Kelly Jo (the second runner-up for the bachelor's affections) says to Lee-Ann that they just want her to be herself, adding "we don't know the real Lee-Ann" and explaining that when she first arrived she was happy and friendly, and then she withdrew from everyone. The next shot is of Kelly Jo saying to the camera (in a different setting) "my experience with Lee-Ann is like [sic] Sybil."[5] She adds, "there are a couple of Lee-Ann's that I know. So, pick one and go with it." This scene confirms Kelly Jo's assessment that Lee-Ann is inconsistent. In this instance, Lee-Ann is seen behaving in a completely opposite way (begging forgiveness) to what we might expect from someone who repeatedly asserts she does not care what others think of her. In addition, Lee-Ann claims she never cries, a statement she repeats in this scene, ironically sobbing as she does so and thus further discrediting herself.

As with Christi, it is Lee-Ann's self-conscious attempt to control herself and to remain in control, and the display of her inability to do so, that reveal her as out of control. The image of Lee-Ann tearful, emotional, and sobbing, contradicts the way she is shown wanting to present herself, implying she is unable to control her emotions. The suggestion is there may be a secret, out-of-control Lee-Ann lurking beneath her cool demeanor, waiting to burst forth.

Bob eventually expresses apprehension about the possible evil that lurks beneath Lee-Ann's attractive exterior. During their one-on-one date on episode four, viewers see a medium shot of Bob and Lee-Ann sitting at a table on the deck of a boat, drinking wine. Bob asks Lee-Ann if she was surprised that the other women voted her least compatible with him. The camera moves to a long shot of the two of them while the audio plays a slow, sharp, high-pitched "plink,

plink, plink" sound, alerting us to danger. As the camera moves in to a close-up of Lee-Ann, she expresses how completely shocked she was. Bob responds, as the camera shots alternate between close-ups of him and Lee-Ann, that he was surprised as well, saying "so it has kind of freaked me out a bit, to me it seems weird" and adding that if people thought they were most compatible at first, he wonders why they then voted her as least compatible with him. The scene cuts to a series of shots of the other women voting for Lee-Ann as least compatible and then back to Lee-Ann saying to Bob, "that's why it has been kinda weird in the house." Bob tries to reassure her by telling her everyone in the house is still her friend. She disagrees. He responds, "regardless, I'm attracted to you and so it doesn't bother me." She says "but you just want to know that I'm the same person when I'm with you. And when I go home I'm not, like, mega-bitch." He says, "that's exactly it," quickly adding that it is important to him that they spend time together.

Here again, as with Christi not wanting to be "*that* girl," Lee-Ann is fully aware of the type of woman she could become ("mega-bitch") that would put her out of the running for the bachelor's affections. As Lee-Ann and Bob articulate, the danger is that Lee-Ann might reveal herself to be someone completely different from the person the bachelor thinks she is. The scenes later on (when Lee-Ann breaks down to Bob and when she breaks down to the women) confirm this is a real threat: Lee-Ann is not who she tries to present herself as, and is not who she sometimes can appear to be. Although Bob and Lee-Ann almost always get along well, the suggestion is that if Bob gets to know the real Lee-Ann (implying that so far he is only getting to know a superficial version of her), she may turn out to be unattractive and frightening. Indeed, right before the next commercial break, the host whets our appetite for what is to come, pinpointing exactly the threat Lee-Ann poses: "and later, Lee-Ann loses control." Part of the impact of the "money-shot" is the self-awareness the women have about the kind of unattractive woman they could appear to be and their express desire not to be that woman. Their downfall is their seeming inability to control their behavior.

Unruly Women

Christi and Lee-Ann take up a lot of space in the seasons in which they appear, and they are disruptive, as are most of the women in the BI who provide money shots. There is potential power in this. Rowe (1997) writes that "through body and speech, the unruly woman violates the unspoken feminine sanction against 'making a spectacle' of herself. I see the unruly woman as the prototype of woman as subject—transgressive above all when she lays claim to her own desire" (p. 76). Rowe continues by saying that

The disruptive power of these women—carnivalesque and carnivalized—contains much potential for feminist appropriation. Such an appropriation could enable us to problematize two areas critical to feminist theories of spectatorship and the subject: the social and cultural norms of femininity, and our understanding of how we are constructed as gendered subjects. (p. 77)

The very image of an unruly, leaky, out-of-bounds woman, in and of itself, is disruptive and offers an opening for a critique. Might the "unruliness" of the women in the BI, women like Christi and Lee-Ann, with their excessiveness, their violation of the codes of femininity, position them to provide a critique of the series and its rigid parameters for appropriate feminine displays? Yes and no.

On the third episode, after Christi's fateful ride on the carousel with Aaron, Christi tells some of the other women in the house that she knows she is not getting a rose. Then, the camera moves closer in on her face as she says "you know, you [the bachelor] told us in the limo that you were looking for someone that would love you despite all your flaws, and that will forgive you for all your mistakes. And you know, the first thing that happens, the first flaw, you like can't get over it. It's just kinda, asking from a girl something you are not able to give." Christi articulates the nuances of the imbalance of power in the harem: the bachelor can disqualify any of the women he perceives as flawed and move on to the many other available women at his disposal. However, if the women want to find love in this context, the bachelor is their only option, flawed or not. Christi spells out the inequality of the setup and the hypocrisy it allows for on the part of the bachelor. However, positioned at this point in the narrative, after viewers see Christi providing numerous "money shots" and after her presentation as aware of her precarious situation (she knows she will not receive a rose), her comments sound like "sour grapes." By the time this scene emerges, the series has presented three episodes in which Christi appears desperately in love with Aaron, frantically wanting to make things "right" but unable to find a way to have her love requited or to fix the situation. The critique of the series is positioned after Christi realizes her defeat, framed as the result of her frustration and exasperation at the situation. Not only does this setup situate Christi as an unreliable source for a critique of the show, it constructs her and most of what she says as unreasonable (the result of what Aaron calls her "unstable" behavior). Christi is not a credible character, and thus neither is her assessment of the situation (similar to how Summer is constructed and how her criticisms of the series are framed, discussed in Chapter 3).

Christi nonetheless offers a poignant image of an unruly woman, that much more poignant because of her awareness of her situation. Perhaps the unwitting result of the series' quest to unravel Christi is a set of images that are powerful regardless of how the series tries to contain them. In some ways, Christi works as a sign of what the series can do to women, that is, make them "crazy," and concomitantly suggests that the BI can be a very unsafe place for women. Nonetheless, the series does a good job of making sense of Christi's unruliness. She appears to be excessive, because that is who she really, truly is (verified by her ability to overcome surveillance and the context of the series to show emotions), try as she might to contain this part of herself.

Lee-Ann is a different story. Some women in the BI cast doubt on the viability of the ideal type of woman the BI promotes by their mere disruptive presence (for instance, Anindita, discussed in Chapter 2). The failure of these women to be contained within the series offers possibilities for the existence of other types of women, that is, women who do not abide by the parameters of the BI. As noted in Chapter 2 in relation to Anindita, the inability of the series to fully shut down these moments of critique and resistance to the overall hegemony of the series offers important glimpses of the mechanism the series uses to construct femininity. This is the case with Lee-Ann.

Lee-Ann addresses the unfair dynamic of the harem structure (several women vying for the attention of one man; the women all at his disposal) and the vulnerable position in which this places the women. Before the rose ceremony at the end of the fourth episode (right before she provides her first "money shot"), Lee-Ann says to the camera, "in a normal situation, if I want a guy, I don't have to see the other nine girls that are going for him. The whole point of this is to be true to yourself. I want to be with Bob. I'm not gonna fake this just so I look like I get along." In the next shot, Karin (an African American woman, discussed in Chapter 2) pulls Lee-Ann aside and says, "I look at you, and I'm, like, you are, like, just such a beautiful girl." Lee-Ann adds, "and I could have any guy I wanted." Karin interjects to agree, saying Lee-Ann can have any guy she wants. Then Lee-Ann says, "so I'm not quivering here waiting for a rose. Grabbing at my heart. And I told myself that when it was not fun, it was over. And I'm not having fun. It was all fun and games until we had a connection [her and the bachelor]." Karin begins to respond, but Lee-Ann interrupts and says, "you want me to behave. So, I'll behave and be miserable for a week. No, I really don't think I should have to share a guy with nine other women. I'm sorry, I'm too good for this sh . . . and if you don't realize that, open your eyes." Karin tells her she just wants Lee-Ann to be prepared for what may happen. Lee-Ann responds, "I'm fine. I'm always fine. Do you ever see me crying? Have you ever seen me cry? I'm true to myself and I'm just not having fun. So, can we please talk about something else? Because I'm so tired of talking about Bob every day of the week." Lee-Ann articulates the disempowering position in which the women are placed. She points to the fact that she (like most of the women on the series) is a desirable commodity in the romance game (she "could have any guy"), and yet she is now in the unenviable position of competing with nine other women for one man. She addresses the hypocrisy of expecting all the women to get along as they chase after the same man. She also articulates a rarely shown perspective on the show: being on the series is "not fun"; it requires women to pretend that they get along with the women against whom they are competing.[6] Finally, she points to the fact that the situation is claustrophobic, creating an environment in which all the women have to talk about is the bachelor.

Lee-Ann pushes her criticism of the series even further. On the same episode in which she tells Karin what she thinks of the situation, she also gives Bob a piece of her mind (right before providing her first "money shot"). Bob sees that Lee-Ann is upset and asks her about it. After some prodding she says, "I mean, really, I'm just hanging in there. No, I'm not having a great time. I guess I'm just not used to waiting for a rose. And I should just be quivering, like. Oh please, there are ten girls here and there are just one of you. And lucky you, you get to make out with every one of us. I'm one of ten girls. And, like, I'm in this for the long run, but I'm not guaranteed anything. So I can spend the week being miserable and one day having fun." After they talk a bit more, he says "I guess I never thought about . . ." she interrupts with "no, I really don't think you do." In this scene, Lee-Ann continues to outline the unfair predicament in which the series, through its harem structure, has placed the women. She also points out that there is very little for the women to gain in this scenario, but that there are a whole lot of benefits for the bachelor. In addition, she gets angry at the bachelor for not considering how the situation makes the women feel, further highlighting his prerogatives: the women spend all their time thinking about him, waiting to spend a minute with him, while he goes around kissing all of them and making all the decisions.

Not only is Lee-Ann given quite a bit of screen time to voice her criticisms, but these, unlike Christi's, do not come across as sour grapes. Rather, Lee-Ann voices these in anger and indignation. Furthermore, while her comments come after many images of her fighting with the other women, they are not the result, as in Christi's case, of knowing she will not receive a rose. In fact, Lee-Ann receives a rose after voicing her thoughts (though she is eliminated the following episode).

Of course, Lee-Ann's inspiring speech is undercut when she begins to cry shortly after delivering it, offering the first of her "money shots" (described earlier). As well, she breaks down tearfully to the other women in the following episode and begs for their forgiveness (providing the second of her "money shots," also described earlier). In this way, the series ultimately undermines her anger and indignation by immediately showing her breaking down tearfully under the pressure, affirming to Bob how much she really cares about him, and telling the women how much she really does care about how they feel about her. These moments reaffirm her commitment to doing well on the series at the same time as they show her being inconsistent. This representation suggests that her anger and indignation do not make her stronger. Quite the opposite: they weaken her. Once she vents her anger, she softens and becomes more vulnerable, which ultimately leads to her undoing because then she is no longer in control of her emotions.

Nonetheless, Lee-Ann's final appearance emphasizes her independence of mind. In the episode "The Women Tell All," the host invites Lee-Ann onstage to speak with Chris, who introduces her by saying "one of the most talked about ladies this season was, of course, Lee-Ann." The requisite montage of clips from her time on the series highlights her ambivalent representation, showing her self-confidence and insistence that she does not care what the other women think about her contrasted with images of her behaving completely differently (crying about how the other women are treating her and apologizing tearfully to them). Of course, there are also many shots of the women talking about how much they dislike Lee-Ann. Predictably, the discussion with Lee-Ann centers on how in-consistent she was in her presentation of self. Fellow-participant Meredith, for instance, says they "just saw two different Lee-Ann's," and another participant comments that Lee-Ann began the season by saying to everyone that she was not aggressive and then proceeded to become the most aggressive woman there.

However, what is most remarkable is Lee-Ann's response to Chris's ques-tion of whether or not she has any regrets. She says yes, she wishes she "had not worn the cream dress" at one of the rose ceremonies and adds "if I could go back, I would have worn the red." Lee-Ann does not resort to the conventional behavior the women are usually shown performing in these moments (discussed in Chapter 5): she does not assert that she knows herself and is proud of the self she presented because it is a consistent self (on the series and in her life); nor does she claim that she has learned from the experience (as Meredith does, dis-cussed in Chapter 5), that she now knows what she needs to improve to do better next time (or do better in life in general). No. In her final moment, Lee-Ann claims that her big regret is about her appearance, asserting that she too can be just as shallow and superficial as the show. With the series trying to pin her down to her original presentation of self, not allowing her the fluidity to occupy several different positions as a woman, Lee-Ann responds in kind, sticking to the most superficial aspect of her presentation of self, her appearance. In this way, she can be read, potentially, as highlighting the shallow and limited nature of the positions afforded women in the BI. In the end, no matter what occurs on the series, it really is all about how the women look.

Closing Thoughts

Grindstaff's discussion of the "money shot" in talk shows moves the "money shot" out of the male domain of film pornography (performed by men, for male viewers), since the shot is provided by women on talk shows and the target au-dience is women. Grindstaff also moves the "money shot" out of the sexual are-na into that of emotions. By using the idea of the "money shot" to discuss the BI, I continue this movement, as the shot is provided by women for a female audience. However, unlike Grindstaff, I root my argument in an examination of the implications of this in a phallocentric context. Borrowing the term "money shot" from film pornography to discuss the construction of fallen women in the

BI opens up the implications of a loss of bodily control, of sexuality and of the exposure of the hidden—of the as-yet-unseen located in the body of a woman. While this combination of elements located in the body of a man in film pornography is meant to be arousing, it becomes explosive and frightening when contained in the body of a woman, revealing a hidden, out-of-control, emotional side and causing an initially attractive woman to immediately lose her appeal.

To be sure, the "money shot" displayed through a female body, as it is in the talk show and in the BI, is antithetical to the original "money shot" in film pornography. To use Williams' terms, the conundrum of the "scientia sexualis" (1993, p. 241) for film pornography is that it is impossible to revel in the "frenzy of the visible" (1989, p. 194) because it is impossible to show the physiology of female sexual pleasure in a heteronormative and phallic visual economy (McClintock, 1993, p. 123; Williams, 1993, p. 242-43). However, the "money shot" in the BI is fully located in the woman and in her female body—but to show an emotional (rather than a sexual) response. Perhaps the "money shot" here illustrates the fear, in mainstream heterosexual U.S. culture, of sexually alluring, intense, and emotional women. Located in the female body, the shot represents anxiety about sexually attractive women losing control of their emotions. This is a tried and true trope for women in popular culture. However, the ingenuity of the "money shot" in the BI is that it disciplines women by enacting a cautionary tale about the dangers of losing control of one's emotions. In so doing, it recruits women into the job of governing the behavior of other women. Women provide the "bad" example (and suffer the consequences) to offer lessons for female viewers on how to properly govern the self. To add punch, the realness of this danger is verified through surveillance. In this way, not only are real women shown displaying real emotions caught on camera, but the emotions are so strong and authentic, so powerful and overwhelming, that not even the fact of surveillance stops the women from displaying them.

Notes

1.   The parallel I draw between film pornography and *The Bachelor* can be extended to talk shows (though this is not a comparison Grindstaff makes).

2.   *The Bachelor* is not unique in its desire to put women on display, to show them as objects of intrigue and mystery and then unravel them. In describing the predicament of women in the mechanical age of reproduction, Berger (1977) writes that women in modern society are taught early on that they are to be surveyed. He argues that women become surveyors of themselves (p. 46). Walters (1995) maintains that "in this society of the spectacle, it is women's bodies that are the spectacle upon which representation occurs [. . .] Women's bodies sell cars, beer; and laundry detergent; women's loves and lives sell soap opera fantasies; women's fears and vulnerability sell blockbuster action films" (p. 22). The display and objectification of women's bodies is omnipresent in popular culture. For more on this, please see the work of Jhally (1995), DuBois, (1988), Kilbourne (1999), and Ewing (1999) (to name a few).

3.   The general camera style on the BI is similar to that of a scripted series. For instance, the lighting is bright. Even at night outside, the scene is well lit. In addition, participants are shot so viewers can see their faces when they speak. The BI sometimes uses a surveillance style for very brief parts of the overnight dates. On these episodes, we see the couple becoming intimate in their hotel room through surveillance-style camerawork. For instance, during Aaron's overnight date with Gwen in season two, viewers spy the couple embrace from the vantage point of a building across from the hotel. We watch through the hotel window, with the aid of a night-vision camera (everything is tinted green).

4.   The decision about who is least compatible with Bob is conflated with who the women dislike the most.

5.   Sybil is probably a reference to the famous case of a woman with sixteen multiple personalities, about whom Schreiber wrote the best-selling 1973 book *Sybil*.

6.   Lee-Ann is critical of the way the women relate to one another in the house and of the expectation that they will get along. On episode three, when all the women but Meredith and Lee-Ann are in tears when voting for the least compatible woman for Bob, Lee-Ann says to the camera, as the music from the *Twilight Zone* television series plays in the background, that the situation is "like a sorority house gone very bad." Later in the same episode, she says to the camera that there are "definitely girls I don't like, so I'm not gonna pretend we are sisters. Oh gag," and she makes a puking motion (pointing her finger toward her open mouth).

Chapter 5: "Therapeutics of the Self"

Reality TV shows often bring together key conventional elements of the therapeutic: self-reflexive comments in displays of the self, and an emphasis on talk and confession. These activities are carried out under surveillance in reality TV. Viewers watch participants talk directly to the camera and to each other about their experiences and about what these experiences have taught them about themselves. Reality television situates surveillance as an explicit technology of confession and elides the editing and production process to affirm agency over presentations of the self (participants often claim the edited and produced version of themselves as a product of their own making). This chapter looks at the interplay of surveillance, confession, and the therapeutic. This is the only chapter that does not focus on gender specifically, though it does focus primarily on female participants. The trope of what I label the "therapeutics of the self" is one way participants are authenticated under surveillance in the BI and thus is enacted primarily by white participants. Little space is given to women of color in the BI to show themselves as authentic (they serve in authenticating the white women).

Self-Expression and Surveillance

Jennifer Ringley's assessment of the role of the Jennicam (Ringley put herself on display on the Internet via a web camera named the "Jennicam") and Andrejevic's (2004) analysis of this phenomena (one of the few scholars to look at reality programming and the therapeutic) nicely open up a discussion of how surveillance is twinned with self-expression and the therapeutic. Andrejevic writes:

Ringley sees herself as an advertisement for the personal benefits of self-disclosure: "I think most of what people go into private to hide—their bodies, their silly habits, their insecurities—is only doing more harm than good by being hidden . . . I'm not doing Jennicam to show the world my details necessarily, but hopefully to show generally that owning up to these things isn't a bad thing, it's great!" Voluntary submission to comprehensive surveillance becomes a therapeutic experience. (p. 86)

These striking assertions by Ringley suggest a notion of the therapeutic that is counterintuitive. Framed in the language of therapy ("insecurities," "owning up to things"), Ringley's articulation of the benefits of the experience of putting herself under surveillance are not, in fact, about how these have transformed or changed her for the better. Rather, the benefits of the experience are that she has exposed her real (private, "true") self, that she has not changed or modified this self under surveillance, that she will proudly display who she "really" is (who she is in private as well as in public), and that her recognition that she has not changed is therapeutic. An improved self, what a therapeutic experience generally signifies, is not the value of the experience Ringley claims. Rather, the value is in the act of exposure and in the display of a consistent self across disparate social spaces (in private and online).

This example helps Andrejevic elaborate his argument about surveillance, the therapeutic, and reality television: participants on reality shows articulate their experiences under surveillance as good because being on the series has been a learning experience with some kind of therapeutic end. Participants leave the show with something that has value, something that has changed them in important ways. Andrejevic (2004) argues that revealing the self under surveillance is a means of proving—verifying—one's self-knowledge and self-awareness, and that this works in a therapeutic capacity (p. 143). He writes, "underlining this euphoric rhetoric of experience is the equation of surveillance with self-fulfillment: that being watched all the time serves to intensify one's experiences, and thereby to facilitate self-growth and self-knowledge" (p. 145). Andrejevic's interest is primarily in surveillance and the work it performs, not in the therapeutic. He aptly pinpoints the experiences of participants, but situates their behavior as falling in line with what has traditionally been outlined as therapeutic. He does not look at how what Ringley articulates is, in many ways, counter-therapeutic, though framed as therapeutic nonetheless. I call this commingling of stasis (not changing the self, asserting self-sameness) and therapeutic transformation, the "therapeutics of the self." I am interested in the implications of this new use of the therapeutic emerging in popular texts, especially ones that use surveillance.

Therapeutics of the Self

Scholars who study the therapeutic in popular culture (among others, White, 1992, 2002; Peck, 1995; Cloud, 1998; Shattuc, 1997) note a trend to constantly incite subjects to work on (change) the self. The "therapeutics of the self" builds on this trend but is significantly different from it. I use the term "therapeutics" because the assertion of the self is often made using paradigms and terms from therapy, implicitly suggesting that affirmation of a consistent (unchanged) self somehow accesses the rewards of a therapeutic transformation: the assertion of a consistent self performs a kind of therapeutic work. In addition, the "therapeutics of the self" is intricately tied to surveillance as a kind of technology of confession, part of a machinery that assists confession, part of the mechanism through which confession occurs.

To illustrate how the "therapeutics of the self" works, I diverge from reality TV briefly to look at a Hallmark e-card,[1] *The Adventures of Phillip the well-adjusted Stink Bug* (www.hallmark.com), because it so aptly illustrates what I am talking about. Clicking on the link for the e-card causes the words "Episode I: All work and no therapy. . ." to scroll across the computer screen followed by an animated cartoon of a bug flying by an upside down paper cup with a cut-out door and a sign over the door that reads "Buggo Industries." The next shot pans across a sea of green cubicles, culminating in a medium shot of Phillip the Stink-Bug, a large animated bug with four arms, a pair of antennae, and a green face poking out of his dapper bow-tie-adorned carapace, sitting behind a desk with a computer in a cubicle decorated with framed pictures of a Dr. Doug. Phillip drinks from his Dr. Doug mug as he sits in front of his computer, on the side of which is a sticker that reads "I ♥ Dr. Doug." Phillip logs onto the website www.ilovedrdoug.bug, which promises personalized online therapy with "Dr. Doug." Eventually, Dr. Doug, a wise-looking, hard-shelled bug of the same genus as Phillip, appears on the computer screen on Phillip's desk. Dr. Doug says "good morning," and then his voice suddenly pauses, wavers, and a monotone automated voice replaces Dr. Doug's voice and says, "Phil-lip?" Phillip raises his Dr. Doug mug and replies "good morning, Dr. Doug!" Dr. Doug asks "are you ready for today's life-affirming activity [automated voice interjects again] Phil-lip?" Phillip replies "oh yes, Doctor." Dr. Doug demands "repeat after me: I am [automated voice] Phil-lip, and I am a [automated voice fills in again] Stii-iiink-B-uu-ug." Phillip, sweat forming on his brow, cowers behind his computer and meekly says "I am Phillip, and I am a Stink-Bug." The doctor entreats, "again!" The shot pulls in from a medium shot to a close-up of Phillip's green face as he says, with a bit more enthusiasm, "I am Phillip, and I am a Stink-Bug." The doctor orders "louder!" As the shot moves in more tightly to his face, Phillip raises his arms in the air and says triumphantly, his voice quavering with emotion, "I am Phillip. I am a stink-bug!" A green mist rises around him as he speaks, and groans emanate from the neighboring cubicles. The last shot is of

Phillip on the right side of the screen, with a bubble above him with the words "Remember, never be afraid of who you are . . . even if you stink."

This e-card vividly illustrates the trend I observe in the BI: the work of therapy is to learn how to affirm oneself confidently (loudly and repeatedly) as Dr. Doug insists Phillip learn to do. Affirming the self is not easy. Phillip must work hard to do this (he sweats, he needs encouragement, it takes several tries to get it right). However, once the self is affirmed, one's "true essence," in this case stinkiness, can come out; and the discomfort of others that can occur (groans from the neighboring cubicles because of the stinkiness) is of little consequence. Therapy comes to be equated with a proud assertion of an unchanged self. The therapeutic change is that Phillip is able to affirm proudly, and loudly, that he is a stink-bug (whereas before he did not take pride in who he was). The e-card holds the promise that learning to assert his stinkiness will transform Phillip therapeutically and help him be a well-adjusted stink-bug. Most importantly, therapeutic gains are realized through affirmation of oneself and a commitment to *not* changing.

To be sure, accepting the self has always been an integral aspect of the therapeutic. Nonetheless, there is also a commitment to changing this self. For instance, while part of the process in the Alcoholics Anonymous model of the therapeutic is to accept the self, what is most important is being vigilant to change the self, to not act on one's essential identity as an alcoholic.[2] The "therapeutics of the self" is a subtle shift from the idea of admitting something "bad" about the self in order to change this "bad" part to an admission of something "good" about the self and an embracing of this—or an admission that one's "true" and authentic self is good (no matter what that self is like), with little attention to changing what might be "bad." There are, of course, several reality TV shows that express conventional notions of the therapeutic, where participants are expected to be transformed from the reality TV experience. This conventional notion exists in the BI as well, alongside the "therapeutics of the self." What I highlight is how the "therapeutics of the self" marks a type of transformation that differs from conventional notions of the therapeutic. Case in point, Phillip the Stink-Bug is learning not to manage his stink (to make his social existence easier, so his colleagues can breathe more easily, for instance), but rather to assert that he will not change his self: he is a Stink-Bug, no matter where he is, what he is doing, or what others may feel about who he is or how he behaves.

Another idea embodied in this e-card is that the therapeutic process need not involve an actual embodied other person. Here the therapist is an automated bug in a computer program. In other words, therapeutic transformation can occur outside a clinical setting and without an embodied therapist.[3] The therapeutic can take place between the self and an absent, imagined other. The interaction with the other is circular in this case, as in some instances in the BI, from the self, back to the self, without passing through a physical, bodily other (to reaffirm the unchanged self). Indeed, White (1992) suggests the therapeutic dynamic, traditionally a "private exchange between two individuals—in a church or a doctor's office, for example" (p. 9), has become, on television, "a public event, staged by the technological and signifying conventions of the television apparatus" (p. 9). In the BI, the television apparatus, coupled with the use of surveillance, creates a virtual other through the edited and produced representations of participants, representations with which participants must interact by watching and commenting on them during episodes taped in a studio before a live audience.[4]

Surveillance and Self-Reflection

Most reality TV shows include scenes where participants articulate assessments of themselves on the programs, often during confessions to the camera and frequently using therapeutic paradigms. In the BI, this happens especially during the episodes "The Women Tell All," "The Men Tell All," and "After the Final Rose," where participants are asked to articulate a final assessment of their actions on the series. Briefly, here are some additional details about these episodes. "The Women/Men Tell All" episode is the second-to-last episode aired in the season, the episode before the finale. Audiences do not yet know who the star has chosen when this episode airs. The "After the Final Rose" episode is the episode that airs after the series ends, at which point the person selected by the bachelor or bachelorette is known. As mentioned, both episodes are in "talk show" format, taped in front of a live studio audience. Participants are interviewed by the host, and audience members can ask participants questions. The episodes are like a "time-out" from the action that season or an opportunity to assess the action, where participants comment directly on their experiences on the series, remark on their presentation of self, and answer questions about their experiences.

Because participants have already viewed aired shows from the season at the time "The Women/Men Tell All," and "After the Final Rose" episodes are aired (the host and participants speak as if this is the case), participants are reflecting on their experience on the series, and evaluating their selves in the shows aired. The act of reflecting on a surveilled representation of themselves is made explicit by the fact that immediately after a participant is invited onstage to speak with host Chris, a montage is screened of clips of the participant in selected moments from aired episodes, and Chris asks the participant to reflect on his or her experiences on the series. The reflections of participants are central to how people articulate their experiences as being therapeutic.

In "The Women Tell All" episode on the second season of *The Bachelor*, third runner-up Gwen, eliminated the previous week, sits on the podium next to the host. We see a medium close-up shot of Gwen as she tells the host in a sometimes wavering voice that as far as she and Aaron are concerned, there are "so many unanswered issues, so many things I'd like to ask him that I don't have clarity on." When asked by Chris if she feels her past divorce was a factor in her not receiving a rose, she answers, "look, it's who I am, it's what made me who I am. I learned a lot from that, and it made me look at who I am and it made me look at relationships." She ends by saying either Aaron likes her as she is, or he doesn't. Gwen affirms that she is comfortable with who she is and that she ultimately loves herself, even if the bachelor does not. Gwen uses therapeutic language to express her sense of self, her pride in herself and her self-knowledge: I have confessed myself adequately, I have shown my emotions, I have revealed my inner feelings, and I have been (on the show) who I truly am in 'real' life, consistently and unchanged. My reward, if nothing else (love), is that I am who I am. While Gwen is eliminated from the season before claiming the bachelor as her prize, she does not go home empty-handed. She claims that she knows who she is, and she appears confident in who she has displayed under surveillance (in essence, confident in how the series has represented her). And this knowledge, the series suggests, will accomplish a therapeutic good.

Bob, one of the participants on the first season of *The Bachelorette* and the starring bachelor on the fourth season of *The Bachelor*, is another person whose experiences are framed as therapeutic. This becomes especially clear in the book he wrote, *What a Difference a Year Makes: How Life's Unexpected Setbacks Can Lead to Unexpected Joy* (2003).[5] The book itself is framed as a therapeutic tool, even though Bob does not explicitly frame his experiences as therapeutic (though implicitly he does). In the introduction, Bob explains that the publisher felt that sharing his experiences "might inspire others who needed help recovering from a broken heart" (p. 3). Bob has learned and grown from the past year of his life (as evidenced by the title of the book), a year marked by a divorce and his appearance in the BI shows. He finds great value in his experiences and hopes others will as well. He says, "if what I learned can help you lift yourself up at a time when you might be feeling a little down, nothing would make me happier" (p. 3). About his impending appearance on *The Bachelor* season four, Bob notes, "who knows? I'm going into it with an honest and open heart, ready to see what happens. If nothing else, it's bound to be a valuable learning experience, just like every other thing that's happened to me over the past year or so" (p. 153). Thus, the idea of growing and learning from his own experiences and teaching others to do the same—therapeutic imperatives—are integral to the premise and content of the book. It is also clear that putting oneself under surveillance for all to see, or publishing a book for all to read, can work therapeutically for those viewing or reading (as well as for the writer/person viewed).

Talk Is Not Enough

When White (1992) charts what she sees as the main imperative of therapeutic discourse in U.S. culture, she notes that the therapeutic is a process that involves constant confession and talk about the self to others. Strategies are the key elements in this process, not arriving at a final resolution or cure. White maintains that "recognition, acknowledgment, and confession of these problems—even to oneself—play a crucial role in the process. In other words, therapy has come to refer to the processes of negotiating and working through one's social subjectivity" (p. 12). The emphasis is on working on the self, and as Shattuc (1997) notes, this involves self-disclosure, an "active decision to overcome shame, guilt, and inhibition" (p. 116). It is only through revealing, confessing, talking about the self that the work of curing oneself can be done. Peck (1995) articulates a similar idea in her discussion of the *Oprah* and *Sally Jessy Raphael* talk shows, noting that "the belief that communication can guide people out of their dilemmas makes these shows compatible with therapeutic discourse" (p. 59). A therapeutic good can come about through talking and communicating with others.

What these articulations of the therapeutic stress is that labor upon the self—through talk, by working through issues, by revealing the self—can transform us for the better, help us overcome what ails us, make us healthier, happier individuals. Thus, in Rieff's words (quoted in Cloud), "the self, improved, is the ultimate concern of moral culture" (Cloud, 1998, p. 31), that is, improving the self, working on the self, is akin to performing one's moral duty. However, these descriptions of the therapeutic cannot explain what Ringley expresses as her therapeutic experience or what I outline above about Gwen and Bob in the BI—that ultimately, whether or not they are the final man or woman, they have earned the reward of knowing who they are and standing proudly by it. The "therapeutics of the self" allows participants who do not win the star's heart to claim a "prize" they can take home with them: knowledge about themselves and confidence in themselves. Participants who fail to claim the "therapeutics of the self" sometimes learn a more conventional therapeutic lesson: they need to change. Specifically, they need to learn to claim self-knowledge and self-confidence.

Surveillance as a Technology of Confession

I reframe Foucault's ideas about confession and the panopticon to extend them to an understanding of surveillance as a technology of confession and of the "therapeutics of the self." While Foucault did not discuss the intersection of confession and surveillance of the self on camera, his elaboration of the historical role of confession is useful in discussing how confession operates in the BI, especially his theorizing on how it is required by an "other." Foucault famously contends that "one does not confess without the presence (or virtual presence) of a partner who is not simply the interlocutor but the authority who requires the confession, prescribes and appreciates it, and intervenes in order to judge, punish, forgive, console, and reconcile" (1990, p. 62). Confession is then a ritual with resistances and obstacles, one that "produces intrinsic modifications in the person who articulates it: it exonerates, redeems, and purifies him; it unburdens him of his wrongs, liberates him, and promises him salvation" (Foucault, 1990, p. 62). Confession is always part of a dynamic between two or more presences—one of which can be virtual. Surveillance fits the same mold: it is always required by an other (virtual or real), someone who will watch. This is particularly true of Bentham's panopticon structure, in which the position of the watcher is literally architecturally central, allowing complete surveillance and making the activities of the panopticon's inhabitants visible at all times to the watcher, who remains invisible to the structure's inhabitants. Without the position of the watcher, there would be no point to the panoptic structure. As Poster (1984) articulates, "the ingenious purpose served by this arrangement was that the prisoner would be conscious of being under continual surveillance" (p. 101).

As discussed in Chapter 1, part of the process of confessing the self in the BI is the awareness of being under surveillance. The narratives are built around how well or poorly participants confess themselves under surveillance: Have they done so well enough to gain access to the rewards of the series? Well enough to claim the "therapeutics of the self"? In some sense, the confession that occurs is from the self to the self (as it passes through the technology of surveillance and through the editing and production process), at least this is explicitly the case on the episodes where participants must contend with the final edited version of their representation on the series and make sense of their presentation of self. Foucault's words, quoted above, are particularly relevant here: "it exonerates, redeems, and purifies him; it unburdens him of his wrongs, liberates him, and promises him salvation" (Foucault, 1990, p. 62). In the BI, it is the representation of the confessed and confessing self under surveillance that does this work, and this is articulated most clearly by participants when they reflect on their tenure on the series.

Though the environment in which the action of a reality show takes place is not panoptic in its architecture, it performs similar work through the use of strategically placed cameras and the knowledge of participants that what they say and do will be on camera. While the camera is always present and "watching" in reality television, in the panopticon it is the sense that someone *could* always be watching that is powerful, though no one may actually be watching. Thus, there is a self-monitoring, a self-policing strategy at work in reality television akin to the work Foucault (1995) outlines the panopticon performing (p. 172). In reality television, however, the surveyor (camera) is always present recording activities even if no one is actually watching, while in the panopticon, it is the threat of being watched that polices the behavior of the surveilled, as there is no recording of activities and someone may or may not be watching.

In the BI shows, and in many reality shows, those inside the surveilled environment are completely visible (first to the crew of the show and then, in an edited version, to the television public and to themselves). Of course, the nature of the structure, the fact that one's every move is recorded by a camera, works to control the activities of participants, to transform them in some sense. Participants know they are being watched and are there to be watched, which serves to regulate their behavior. Participants self-regulate based on the demands and parameters of the context. Most important, however, their behavior is literally disciplined through the production and editing process, which makes "it possible to know them, alter them" (Foucault, 1995, p. 172). While Foucault (1995) suggests that "stones can make people docile and knowable" (p. 172), cameras and the subsequent production and editing of surveilled images used to produce reality television can have the same effect.

Foucault did not discuss the prisoners' attitudes in relation to surveillance. However, participants in the BI do at times discuss their feelings about being surveilled (Heather, discussed in Chapter 1, says "I've never really gotten my heart broken, and to get it broken on national TV is just, like, killer"). More importantly, the very structure of certain episodes ("The Men/Women Tell All," "After the Final Rose") implicitly insists that participants reflect on their experiences while being surveilled, since they must comment on a representation (montage of clips) of themselves under surveillance. In the BI, all that is surveilled can be used to confess the self, and all that is selected during the editing and production process can be used to represent a confessed self.

Mediating the Self: Authentic Selves on TV

The process of surveillance, production, and editing in the BI are part of a mechanism that makes people knowable to themselves and to others and subsequently has the potential to carry out a therapeutic good. Confession, as Dovey (2000) suggests, has become an important practice in the "quest for psychic health, as part of our 'right' to selfhood" (p. 107). If we add to this the notion of surveillance as used on reality TV shows, this quest passes through the technology of surveillance, through the editing and production process, and through a public reformulation by participants (of the representation of their selves on the series) in an edited and produced version of the surveillance footage. Thus, while participants in the BI articulate the "therapeutics of the self" as an accomplishment realized by revealing their "true" and real self, the process is highly mediated and regulated by the technology of surveillance and by the production and editing process involved in creating a television text. Indeed, participants do not, in fact, have complete autonomy in how they present their selves under surveillance (though they often claim to). What is elided in this mediated presentation of participants is how the editing and production process factors into the equation. For instance, during the montage sequences on the episodes, no mention is made of the process of putting together the montage (involving many choices by workers on the show), let alone the process of putting together each episode in the series. It is through interaction with a mediated virtual other (the participants themselves in the montage and on the aired episodes) that the series shows participants learning to affirm the self. In other words, participants are never entirely in control of how they are presented in the BI. In fact, for the most part they have no control at all over how they are presented.

The ways that surveillance, confession, production and editing are integral to the "therapeutics of the self" are evident in the "After the Final Rose" episode of season five of *The Bachelor*. The host speaks with Tara, runner-up for the affections of bachelor Jesse. After bringing her onstage, he introduces a montage of clips, imploring Tara to watch her "journey on the bachelor" (words used on most episodes to introduce a montage of clips of a participant), suggesting that this edited montage represents the entirety of her time on the series and, concomitantly, her real self. This montage serves as the opening to a conversation about how Tara feels about her appearance on the series. After the montage, the host turns to Tara and tells her that everyone watched her and the bachelor falling in love slowly, and that although it took Tara a long time to open up to the experience, everyone saw that she finally did. The host asks Tara if she loved the bachelor? Tara affirms she did, adding that she was extremely happy and would have accepted a proposal. The host comments that one of the remarkable things people noticed about her is how clearly she spoke her mind to the bachelor. He then asks if she is proud of how she handled things. Tara says "it's not necessarily that I'm proud of it. I just think that's who I am. If I have something to say to somebody, I'm gonna say it . . ." The host interrupts to comment that he found it sad when she said that these kinds of things always happen to her. Tara acknowledges that she's always in relationships that don't work out for awful reasons. The host comments that on the final night on the show he was under the impression the bachelor managed to get away with saying very little and that she did most of the talking. Tara laughs as she says she put everything on the table that night, leaving nothing unsaid.

By having Tara comment on her experiences immediately after showing a montage of these, the show situates her not only as commenting on the representation of herself but also as affirming that this representation is real, confirming a consistency between how she is represented on the series and who she is in real life— "I just think that's who I am. If I have something to say to somebody, I'm gonna say it." Tara adds that events on the show were consistent with how things happen in her life (that she's always in relationships that never work out), but most importantly, she confirms that the entire process of the BI (surveillance, editing, production) can do the work of representing a real and consistent self.

As well, the series shows Tara demonstrating very little self-consciousness about the constructed nature of her moments in the final television product. In commenting on her presentation of self on the series, Tara is in fact reflecting upon the process of surveillance and of mediation—how well she appeared under surveillance, how well she confessed through the technology of surveillance, and how well she was represented through the editing and production process. Television is used to verify the self as authentic, and production, editing, and all the work that goes into creating a show becomes a natural way of authenticating the self under surveillance. Concomitantly, television works as a therapeutic tool: the verification of authenticity under surveillance instills confidence that one is always consistent, and knowledge (and proof) of this results in a therapeutic good.

Consistency Across Disparate Spaces

In the Ringley example and in the BI, people affirm a surveilled representation of their self, one that privileges consistency across disparate social spaces. In the space of reality TV, this means insisting that who one is in the clips, on the aired episodes, onstage, and in one's real life, is who one "really" is. As discussed in Chapter 1, often there is an affirmation of consistency between who one appears to be under surveillance on the series and who one is imagined to be in one's real life (off-camera). Surveillance is central in this setup, because it is in acknowledging the surveilled image of oneself (publicly, under surveillance) that people are able to confirm that this is who they really are, what they are actually like in their daily lives off-camera. Case in point, most of Bob's book has the implicit aim of showing that Bob is always consistent in his behavior—thus unchanged. Bob repeatedly affirms that the assertion of a consistent self is important. He writes:

> I had been myself on the show, and that was the important thing. I've never tried to pretend I'm something I'm not. It isn't hard for me to act natural, because who I am at heart has been pretty much unchanged since I was a kid. I'm not a complicated person. I have never taken myself too seriously, and that's the way I was on the show. (Guiney, 2003, p. 134)

Bob maintains that while on *The Bachelorette* he never pretended to be someone he was not, that he always acted naturally and that he remains consistent as a person—unchanged since he was a kid. Toward the end of the book, he writes, "people often ask my friends how all this media attention has changed me, and I've heard them say it hasn't changed me at all—and that's a huge compliment" (p. 143). Bob's claim to have learned so much over the past year, coupled with assertions about his ability to be himself at all times, especially during his tenure on *The Bachelorette* (and his expectation that he will act the same way as the star of *The Bachelor*), suggest that part of what he has learned is how to affirm a consistent self and that learning to do this will yield a therapeutic result—help him live a better life, transform him in ways that enable him to move on from the sadness of his divorce (and help others do the same). Bob's book is both an expostulation on how much he has been transformed for the better by his experiences during the past year and an elaboration of how he has remained true to himself, been the same all his life—about how much he has *not* changed. The paradox in these conflicting assertions is the paradox at the heart of the "therapeutics of the self": consistency is affirmed as a means of producing therapeutic transformation.

Trish's behavior on the fifth season of *The Bachelor* is a striking example of the importance of consistency and the valorization of the ability to be consistently one's true self, no matter how unpleasant that self might be. The creators paint Trish as the villainess of the season. On the first episode, before Trish is introduced, the host warns that she will be the most hated bachelorette ever. In "The Women Tell All" episode, the host describes her as the "most despised woman in bachelor history." However, while Trish is presented as a dislikeable woman, she is lauded for being unabashedly her real self at all times and emerges as admirable for this ability. Like Phillip the stink-bug, she may be unpleasant to be around, but she is worthy of admiration because she proudly refuses to change to make herself easier to be around.

The series gives Trish center stage, and she becomes embroiled in most of the narrative action even long after she is eliminated. In an unprecedented move, producers bring Trish back to the show, after she is eliminated the previous week, to try to win back the bachelor (he turns her down). In "The Women Tell All" episode, the host interviews Trish first, and her interview lasts as long as that of the most recently eliminated woman, who usually gets the longest interview (Trish was eliminated two episodes earlier), and as long as the interview with the bachelor. Trish figures prominently in most of the discussions on this episode, even when she is no longer on stage. Many of the questions posed to participants are about their feelings about Trish. In another unusual move, the series brings Trish on stage in the "After the Final Rose" episode. Generally, the only participants who appear on this episode are the second runner-up, the final woman or man chosen by the star of the season, and the star. Indeed, the episode opens with a "candid" behind-the-scenes discussion between Trish and the host about her plans to confront a fellow-participant, second runner-up Tara (discussed above).

Once Tara and Trish are brought together on stage, a montage of clips of each woman talking about the other is shown. In sum, Tara calls Trish a "slut," "pond scum," "unattractive," and "disgusting" and says Trish has "no morals or values." Trish calls Tara a "spoilt and sheltered brat" and "a bitch," and says Tara "spits venom," is "too young," "insecure," is "ugly on the inside," has a lot of "issues," and puts up a "good front" but is "not nice" behind the scenes. The discussion on stage centers not on the specific comments made by each of the women but rather on whether they have presented consistent selves on the series, hence giving Trish the advantage.

Trish accuses Tara of saying things behind Trish's back and of being two-faced, of acting nice, prim, and proper in one setting, but being completely different in another. Trish claims she is a better person because she can stand by what she has said on camera: "I've been the same person the entire time on this show and in my life. I am the same person." Tara retorts that she also stands by who she was on camera, asserting that she speaks her mind and thinks there is nothing wrong with this. Trish shoots back that Tara only does this behind other peoples' backs, saying this is the difference between them. Trish accuses Tara of going out of her way to say mean things behind her back—something Trish claims she never did. Trish adds: "I'm sorry . . . you radiate unhappiness. I know who I am and I like who I am."

Trish's last statement ("I'm sorry . . . I like who I am") illustrates how knowledge of the self and the ability to assert a consistent self under surveillance translate into performing a therapeutic good. Trish equates what she perceives to be Tara's unhappiness with her inability to be consistently herself under surveillance, and equates her own satisfaction with herself and her knowledge of herself with her being consistent under surveillance. The display of a consistent self is articulated by Trish as a healthy self, indeed a therapeutic self, allowing her to know and like who she is. While Trish clearly failed to access the explicit rewards of the series (finding love), and while she is represented as disliked by virtually everyone on the show, the focus is not on the kind of self that has been represented but on whether this self is consistent and real under surveillance—that is, consistent on the series with who Trish is in real life.

The series gives Trish substantial air time to assert the "therapeutics of the self" and to receive kudos from fellow-participants for her ability to display a consistent and real self under surveillance. Jean-Marie, another participant, says during "The Women Tell All" episode:

> I commend Trish. [And says to Trish] This is the only thing I commend you for, is being who you are . . . be who you are, and this is what I commend you for the whole time. You said I want this, this is what I want, don't fold in now honey, if that's who you are, stick with it.

Another bachelorette on this same episode, DeShawn, says of Trish that "she's completely held her ground, stood by who she is" even if others didn't like who she was or agree with the things she did. Furthermore, when asked by host Chris for her thoughts on Trish, Jenny (who lives with the women for a few weeks, pretending she is vying for the bachelor's affections when really she is a friend of the bachelor's and is spying on the women), says she feels Trish is the wrong person for the bachelor because Trish does not have the right values to make a good wife for him. In other words, Trish is unsuitable for the bachelor because she is truly a bad match for him, which Jenny's sleuthing confirms.

Because Trish has been able to affirm a consistent self—she affirms it in how she assesses her representation on the series and this is confirmed by fellow-participants—she can ultimately feel good about the self confessed under surveillance, even if it is one nobody likes and one that is not a suitable match for the bachelor. Conversely, Tara, who the series depicts as being liked by fellow-participants, does not fare well on this episode because she is unable to defend a consistent self. Indeed, viewers actually see her leaving the stage shortly after the above exchange with Trish, refusing to defend her presentation of self, refusing to claim the "therapeutics of the self." Tara agrees to return to the stage only to complete the final segment of the show but not to continue her exchange with Trish.

Consistency and Conventional Notions of the Therapeutic

Meredith, contender for the bachelor's affections on season four of *The Bachelor* and star of season two of *The Bachelorette*, displays a more classic sense of the therapeutic. She needs to change herself to become a better person, a happier person, which here means being able to find love. When she appears on *The Bachelor*, as discussed below, she makes the mistake of not letting her seemingly authentic self emerge, keeping it under wraps. Her take-away lesson is about consistency, about learning to be consistent under surveillance with who she is imagined to be in her real life. In the episode "The Women Tell All" from season four of *The Bachelor*, the host invites fourth runner-up Meredith, eliminated from the show the previous week, onstage to be interviewed. A montage of moments from Meredith's tenure on the show is aired (including a clip when she finds out her grandmother passed away). One scene is of Meredith in the limousine after she has been eliminated telling the camera she blames herself for not getting a rose.

After viewing the montage, the host comments to Meredith that it is unusual to see a participant blame herself for not getting a rose,[6] to which Meredith responds that she was, at the time, unable to take the necessary risk (of showing her emotions) to find love. She recounts that she cared about the bachelor as much as the other women but was unable to open up as much as she needed to let him know how she felt. She recounts how the experience was very difficult for her, that she's sorry she got her heart broken. She describes how she sobbed uncontrollably on their first date (after finding out her grandmother had passed away), adding "it's not really normal, I have to say," and asserting that the bachelor made her feel better. The host comments: "it seems like you've learned something about yourself. Is it going to change the way you go about things in the future?" Meredith responds "yeah. I think that in order to find anyone, to allow myself to open up, you have to be open. And, cuz I'm never gonna find anyone if I act the way I did on *The Bachelor*—so I have learned a lot (laughing) . . . It was my fault, and nobody's to blame but myself."

This scene affirms the economy of emotion necessary on the show and the need to take the risk of showing one's emotions for the sake of love. Meredith did not show a proper economy with regard to her feelings for Bob because she was too withholding. The scene also defines how a participant should behave to succeed on the show: not the way Meredith did. Notably, Meredith appears quite open on the series, displaying a lot of emotion and feeling. The problem seems to be that this was in relation to her grandmother's passing and not, as she says, consistent with her behavior when she is her "normal" self. She was in mourning, not who she is in her everyday life, that is, not the self she needs to be to fall in love. All is not lost, however, because Meredith frames this as a learning experience, promising she will do better next time.

What has Meredith learned though? That there are right and wrong kinds of selves for finding love: a self in mourning is definitely the wrong kind of self. She learns she must display, under surveillance, a self consistent with who she is in her real life or who she is imagined to be under normal circumstances. The assumption Meredith makes is that if she had displayed her real "normal" self under surveillance and not her self in mourning (somehow not a real self), she would have ended up with the bachelor. There is no question about her compatibility with Bob or about the circumstances of the show—and concomitantly, the surveillant aspect—being difficult ones in which to fall in love; rather, it is a question of being consistent, on the show and in real life, knowing who one is and proudly displaying this self under surveillance, no matter what.

Meredith does indeed learn her lesson well. She is the star of the second season of *The Bachelorette,* where she becomes skilled at displaying a consistently real and "normal" self under surveillance and is rewarded by finding love (briefly—the couple split after a few months) with her chosen man, Ian.

Therapeutizing the Political

What do we make of participants professing they have been therapeutically transformed by not changing? Bob, Gwen, Tara, and Trish's articulation of their experiences in the BI run counter to the logic of the therapeutic, which demands that the self be transformed as a means of gaining happiness. I am not suggesting traditional notions of the therapeutic do not occur in the BI. Participants certainly do at times maintain a focus on changing the self (Meredith, for instance). While I have not explored this in detail, there are indeed moments when participants enact therapeutic behavior in the BI, such as Jayne in season six of *The Bachelor*, who learns she must be less shy to find love, and Haily and Angela (discussed in Chapter 3) from season two of *The Bachelor*, who learn they need to be more open about their feelings if they want to find love. The "therapeutics of the self" and more conventional notions of the therapeutic can occur at the same time. They are not mutually exclusive.

There is something at stake in the movement from more conventional notions of the therapeutic to the "therapeutics of the self." An essential component of the arguments made by White, Peck, Cloud, and Shattuck about the therapeutic involves what Peck calls the "therapeutic ethos" (Lears, 1983; Bellah et al., 1996, Illouz, 1991; Grodin, 1991; White, 1992): "The use of the individual psyche to explain social phenomena, and the belief that social problems can be resolved with psychological management . . . [which reflects] what critics have identified as a 'therapeutic ethos' in contemporary American culture" (Peck, 1995, p. 58). Peck (1995) argues that "therapeutic discourse translates the political into the psychological; problems are personal (or familial) and have no origin or target outside one's own psychic processes" (p. 75-76). The problem is the turning of the political into the personal. As Cloud (1998) states, "what were once political movements have become translated into personal quests for fulfillment" (p. xii). Cloud refers to this as a "therapeutic discourse," a "rhetorical strategy of offering therapeutic consolation as a substitute for political and economic compensation, [which] has become a commonplace diversion from political engagement in contemporary American society" (p. xi). This is in line with the notion of a "therapeutic ethos."[7] For Cloud, the quest in the therapeutic is to improve the self, to turn attention inward rather than outward, to take one's happiness into one's own hands by working on the self.

Specifically, according to Cloud (1998), the work one must perform on the self involves healing, coping, and adapting (p. xiv). For instance, Cloud cites an example in which "in response to what Susan Faludi has called an antifeminist backlash in popular culture and politics, feminist activist Gloria Steinem came out with a new plan for a 'revolution from within' based on self-esteem" (p. xii).[8] Thus to cure our culture of antifeminism, we need to work on feeling better about ourselves, bolster our self-esteem. In Cloud's words, "we can view the therapeutic as having restorative and conservative effects in the face of conflict and change" (p. xiv). Peck (1995) uses a neo-liberal framework to explain how placing the onus for change on the shoulders of the individual implies that working on the self means participating in a democratic culture, exercising individual freedom. The self improved, then, is not the only concern. Implicit in the move to work on the self is the idea that in so doing one is fulfilling one's democratic right to exercise freedom: we become entrepreneurs of the self rather than social and political activists. White (1992) shares these concerns as well, articulating them as they exist on television: the discourse of therapy on TV is dangerous because it emphasizes a focus on the self as a way of freeing the self, without any vectors leading to social or political transformation.

Stasis as Therapeutic Transformation

The theorists discussed above suggest that therapeutic discourse in Western culture represents a turning inward to the self to find solutions to problems and a turning away from political and economic structures: improving the self to live a happier existence. While these scholars argue that the ideas about change and transformation implicated in the therapeutic are problematic (because the emphasis is on the self to the exclusion of larger political and social issues), they do not examine how sameness and consistency across disparate social spaces, and the proud assertion of these under surveillance—as seen in the Ringley example, the Philip the Stink-Bug e-card, and the BI—are being constructed as a therapeutic good, which I argue further instantiates a focus on the self to the exclusion of all else.

We need to expand notions of the therapeutic to include the idea of affirming self-sameness across disparate social spaces and the use of surveillance to verify sameness. This is becoming part of contemporary therapeutic discourse in the United States, a trend we can see clearly in many reality shows. This trend may be a symptom of a shift on TV from valorization of a therapeutic self to valorization of a consistent self, or to valorization of a consistent self as therapeutic. Thus in the BI, the representation of the self unchanged (unapologetically so) comes to embody idealized therapeutic change.

This shift is significant. Peck (1995) outlines that "therapeutic discourse proposes that we change ourselves without conceding that our identities and actions are determined by social conditions that will not change just because we interpreted and handled them differently on an individual basis" (p. 75). However, in the "therapeutics of the self," the suggestion is not only that we not focus on the social conditions of our existence, but that we *not* change our selves, since a verified and affirmed consistent and unchanged self brings about a therapeutic transformation. The "therapeutics of the self" works to keep people content exactly as they are—to stop any impetus for change, to equate not changing with an important experience that can transform the self for the better.

Contentment with social, political, and economic structures is the consequence of traditional notions of therapeutic discourse and of the "therapeutics of the self," but the "therapeutics of the self" adds a new layer to this by advocating solely for self-knowledge and acceptance. The therapeutic impetus in the "therapeutics of the self" is the *process* of affirming the self: the end result is less important. If we learn to be happy with the self as it is, to love this self, then it does not matter what that self is actually like. This is a step beyond what Peck (1995), Cloud (1998), White (1992, 2002), and Shattuc (1997) note, and moves us further into stasis, but this time on *both* the political and the personal front.

Notes

1.   This is an electronic card sent over e-mail. The person to whom the card is sent is provided with a weblink that brings them to a personalized message from the sender using animation, photographs, or drawings.

2.   In AA, the twelve steps to recovery emphasize the need to admit there is a problem (drinking), one that causes many other problems, and to commit to fixing this problem.   Details   about   the   twelve   steps   can   be   found   online   at http://www.aa.org/lang/en/en_pdfs/smf-121_en.pdf.

3.   For instance, the clinical psychoanalytic dynamic is predicated on the narrative the patient builds with the analyst. Ricoeur (1978) writes "that psychoanalytic theory . . . is the codification of what takes place in the analytic situation and, more precisely, in the analytic relationship. It is there that something happens which merits being called the analytic experience" (p. 185).

4.   The viewer in this setup also occupies the place of the therapist.

5.   Two participants on the second season of *The Bachelor*, Helene Eksterowicz, the final woman the bachelor selects (as discussed in Chapter 4, they break up shortly after the finale), and Gwen Gioia, the third runner-up (the same Gwen discussed in this chapter), published an advice book entitled *Nobody's Perfect: What To Do When You've Fallen for a Jerk But You Want to Make It Work* (2004). Bob, Gwen, and Helene believe their experiences in the BI can be turned into a product that will help others (potentially therapeutically).

6.   This is actually fairly common. For instance, both Haily and Angela (season two of *The Bachelor*), discussed in Chapter 3, blame themselves for their failings on the series.

7.   I have not focused on the nuances in meaning of the different terms ("therapeutic ethos" and "therapeutic discourse"). Peck uses both terms without distinction. I privilege the term "therapeutic discourse," because it suggests a Foucauldian notion of discourse: the therapeutic as a set of practices. For more on the therapeutic in Western culture, please see the work of Bellah, Madsen, Sullivan, Swindler and Tipton (1996); Ben-Yehuda (1990); Cancian (1987); Cushman (1995); DeFranciso, Leto and O'Connor (1995); Ehrenreich and English (1978); Gergen (1991); Grodin (1991); Kaminer (1992); Katz (1993); Lasch (1979, 1984); Payne (1989); Rapping (1996); Riessman and Carroll (1995); Schilling and Fuehrer (1993); Simonds (1996, 1992); Starker (1989); White (1992).

8.   Some scholars note the connection between the self-help movement and neoliberal politics (Ouellette, 2004; Cruikshank, 1996; Rimke, 2000), suggesting that the self-help movement encourages people to learn to take care of themselves and behave as good citizens, to self-discipline. Rapping's insightful work *The Culture of Recovery: Making Sense of the Self-Help Movement in Women's Lives* (1996) makes important links between the self-help movement and the women's consciousness-raising movement in the United States, suggesting that the self-help movement borrowed much from the women's movement, especially in regards to notions of empowerment. Rapping comments that while the women's movement is about identifying a personal malaise for women and finding the social cause of this problem, the self-help movement is about identifying a personal malaise and finding a personal solution to this problem (curing the self through work on the self). Steinem inverts this by pointing to the self-help movement to resolve problems traditionally addressed by the women's movement via social and political activism.

Chapter 6: Empowerment and Choice in the Postfeminist Nirvana

Reality TV promises that at least part of what is seen in the final product will stem from unplanned and unscripted spontaneous moments, even if the context for these might be understood to be constructed. Nonetheless, as I've been suggesting throughout, what occurs in the space of a reality TV show is often highly regulated to produce specific outcomes. This chapter looks at how the BI is regulated to privilege a particular type of woman, and how feminist-seeming notions of choice and empowerment figure into the equation.

The BI is set up to suggest that the women are culled from the everyday world and that the shows are just one place among many to meet women and find love. For example, in the introductory episode of season three of *The Bachelor*, bachelor Andrew responds to the host's question about why he chose the show as a way of finding love by saying "there's no handbook on how to find true love," suggesting *The Bachelor* is as good and normal a route to finding love as any other. In the introductory episode to season four of *The Bachelor*, bachelor Bob responds to the same question by stating that the show is a great opportunity to meet twenty-five people he might not otherwise meet, articulating the show as simply a context for meeting more people (not for meeting particular types of women). In the second episode of season five of *The Bachelorette*, star Jillian, also a participant on season thirteen of *The Bachelor*, explicitly emphasizes her "ordinariness," saying to the camera that she is just an "average girl," not a "skinny blond" "model-type" with "big boobs." In her words, she's a "quirky little brown-haired Canadian."

However, Jillian, like the other women in the BI, fits a consistent type of woman selected who "reinforces current U.S. standards of female beauty and objectification of the woman's body" (Yep and Camacho, 2004, p. 339). A snapshot of the women at just about any rose ceremony on the series reveals that these are not ordinary women. They are glamorous and well primped (the rose ceremony is one among many events on the series where the women need to look dressed-up). They wear expensive, fully accessorized evening gowns, their hair impeccably styled and their makeup flawlessly applied. To enter this contest, a woman must have the raw material to achieve this look. For instance, a woman who is a size twelve or four feet ten inches tall will never look like the women on the series. She would need to be a size six, or preferably (ideally) a size four or smaller, and she would have to be of average height (a little shorter or taller than what is normally seen on prime-time television will do as well) and have no visible physical disabilities. As well, raw material notwithstanding, she must be willing to spend time donning the proper attire and doing the necessary primping for each moment on the series (even "casual" moments require some preparation to look the way these women look in jeans and a T-shirt).[1]

The stated selection criteria for the women add insight to what is visually apparent. In "The Bachelor Revealed," a special that aired prior to the first episode of the second season of *The Bachelor*, the host outlines the criteria for choosing the twenty-five women.[2] His words are interspersed with images of auditioning women (many in bikinis) and sound bites of women's voices illustrating what he has just said: "If you guys can find Mr. Right for me, why hesitate?" "I would really like to be incredibly famous," "I'm a strategic planner," "I'm ready to meet somebody and to settle down," and "I want a commitment." Chris outlines the criteria:

> The show is called *The Bachelor*, but the women are really the stars. So, picking the right twenty-five women is very important, and it isn't easy. We are searching for twenty-five exceptional women. We organized an all-out hunt to find some of the greatest single women in the country. While many women are nervous, mostly they are excited at the chance to meet the man of their dreams. Trying to find the right ladies for the bachelor is a huge undertaking. The casting department considers everyone that applies. They scrutinize every aspect of the bachelorette candidate. She must be single, between the ages of twenty-one and thirty-five. She must be adventurous, ready for marriage. She should be intelligent. She should be ambitious. And of course, attractive. The forty women are then put up in hotel rooms, where, just like the bachelor candidate, they go through medical exams, psychological tests, and extensive background checks. The producers then videotape in-depth interviews with the women to determine if they want to be on the show for the right reason, and that reason is marriage.

A woman wins a spot on the series because she is (out of all the women who apply) "exceptional," which here means "young," "single," "adventurous," and "attractive." She must also have a strong desire to be married to a man. Of course, a woman has a leg up on the competition if she is "ambitious" and "intelligent," but this is not a primary requirement—as the host says, "she *should* be intelligent" "she *should* be ambitious" not "she must be" (as is the case for the other requirements).

Unspoken criteria for the women are that they are heterosexual (Yep and Camacho, 2004) (the women are there to be with the bachelor, not each other) and middle-class (educated and able to have professional careers, discussed shortly)—as these are largely the types of women chosen for the series. A white subject is unproblematically assumed, as discussed in Chapters 1 and 2.

The speech Chris makes to the women before the first rose ceremony on the first episode of season four of *The Bachelor* is telling of how those selected for the show are expected to feel about this honor. The host says:

> Good evening. (Twenty-five women respond in unison "good evening.") Congratulations on being here, and welcome to your first rose ceremony. I have fifteen long-stemmed roses. Each one, of course, represents another woman Bob would like to get to know better. Now I know you all came here specifically to meet Bob. But I want to tell you, you are all totally empowered here. After getting to talk to him and getting to know him a bit better, if Bob is someone you would not consider marrying, you can, and should reject his invitation. I wish you all the best. If you're ready, I'll go get our bachelor. (Chris Harrison, Season Four, Episode One, *The Bachelor*)

Chris makes clear that arriving at this moment is an accomplishment, one worthy of congratulations, something for which the women have worked hard. The final twenty-five women have beaten out many other competitors[3] and undergone extensive testing to be selected—this is a competition, with winners and losers. Chris makes the competitive aspect of the show explicit on the second episode of season twelve when he tells the women that the fifteen women were chosen from thousands who wanted to be on the show. The women who make the final cut are winners and should feel empowered.

When it came to choosing the stars of the six seasons of *The Bachelorette*, the producers invariably selected white women who look like starlets (despite Jillian's claim that she's "just an average girl"). In two instances, the women also have professions or hobbies that require them to look the part: Trista (star of the first season) is a physical therapist and a Miami Heat dancer; and Meredith (star of the second season) is a makeup artist, model, and aspiring chef. Of course, all six stars of *The Bachelorette* first appeared on *The Bachelor* and had therefore, by the time they starred on *The Bachelorette*, already met the criteria outlined by Chris for the women on *The Bachelor*.

The women the men meet in the BI are not women they are likely to meet in the everyday world.[4] When Chris congratulates the women, he is not just congratulating them on their success in the interviews and in the many psychological and physical exams. He is congratulating them on being born with a particular body type and being willing to do the work necessary to achieve and maintain a certain look. These women are fortunate to have been born with the physical attributes of a starlet, if not a model (some are too curvy, or too short to be models)—or at the very least with physical attributes that, if worked on carefully, will allow them to resemble one.

Another precondition of being part of the BI is demonstration of a certain attitude about being filmed: the women must be willing to be on display, objectified, what Mulvey ([1975] 1992) might define as presented as a "spectacle" to be looked at. This requirement is explicit. If the barrage of scenes of bikini-clad women doing all manner of things—from jumping on trampolines, to lying in the sun, sitting in hot tubs and frolicking about—is not enough to signal that the show relies on images of women willingly displaying their scantily clad bodies, the producer of the show, Mike Fleiss, makes this explicit on the first episode of season four of *The Bachelor*: "We take all kinds of things into consideration . . . their psych exams, blood tests. . . . most importantly, they have to look good in a hot tub." This comment is predictably followed by a montage of shots of women in hot tubs, emerging from pools, and laying in the sun in bikinis, and a series of close-ups of the women's body parts (cleavages, bottoms, and legs).

Postfeminism

Postfeminist discourse is helpful in further articulating the requirements for the women in the BI. I use the term "postfeminism" to mean a reactionary discourse that suggests there is no longer a need for feminist action. I do not use the term as it is sometimes academically understood to mean third-wave feminism or a kind of postmodern feminism (Brooks, 1997; Gamble, 1999; Lotz, 2001; Mann, 1997). One of the tropes in postfeminist discourse is that choosing femininity and desiring the male gaze are empowering because these are under a woman's control. Projansky (2001) calls this behavior "heterosexually attractive bodily behavior" (p. 79), which attaches to commodified behavior, to notions of empowerment through choice, aligning heterosexual femininity with feminism. Projansky writes:

> This celebration of women's play with the heterosexual male gaze—their invitation of the gaze and their own fascination with and attention to the object of that gaze (their own bodies)—not only intensifies heterosexuality within the postfeminism depicted in the popular press, but it also ensures a place for femininity in postfeminism. Advertising, in particular, contributes to this version of postfeminism, celebrating women's "equality" and their access to "choice" (feminism), while marketing commodities that call for and support constant body maintenance (femininity). (p. 80)

A link is forged between personal freedom and working on one's appearance. The display of one's body is articulated as a way for women to exercise control and in so doing verify themselves as independent and disciplined (Goldman, Heath and Smith, 1991, p. 338). Hence, "sexuality appears as something women exercise by choice rather than because of their ascribed gender role" (Goldman, Heath and Smith, 1991, p. 338). Shaping one's body into an ideal that will attract the male gaze is "taken as evidence of achievement and self-worth" (Goldman, Heath and Smith, 1991, p. 338), an accomplishment, and not as conforming to the pressure of sexist ideals. Choosing this comportment is cast as an active and empowered choice a woman makes, an "articulation of agency" (Probyn, 1993, p. 278).

The act of choosing is central, rather than the choices to which women have access: I make these choices and nobody else makes them for me. Probyn (1993) defines this as "choiceoisie," the part of postfeminist discourse that couples the notion of choice with feminist imperatives, without considering the "material dictates of class, race, age and sexuality" (p. 278). "Choiceoisie" is envisioned as a replacement for feminism, a way of seeing decisions as individual choices instead of as culturally sanctioned and determined (Helford, 2000, p. 292). Choice is individualized, devoid of any of the implications and responsibilities of choosing. Walters (1995) notes, in quoting Rapp, that this is a depoliticization that "often takes the form of the reduction of feminist *social* goals to individual 'lifestyles'" (p. 137). Individualism is encouraged, to the detriment of community activism (Helford, 2000, p. 292). In postfeminist discourse, women have a range of choices they can make (have a career, vote, have an abortion), but they simply choose not to opt for the choices for which women have fought so hard. Instead, women choose to be married and have children, a choice presented as the realization of a natural desire (Helford, 2000, p. 292). This is "feminism shorn of its political program—choice freed of the necessity of thinking about the political and social ramifications of the act of choosing" (Probyn, 1997, p. 134). This notion of choice is similar to how race is presented, as discussed in Chapter 2, where the starring bachelor's consistent final choice of a white woman is framed as a personal choice, shorn of the imperatives of the raced context of the BI where whiteness is privileged.

In postfeminist discourse, choices are made self-consciously and actively—to fight against a restrictive (i.e., "feminist") notion of what it means to be a strong, independent woman. In this time of backlash, Walters (1995) suggests, feminists are positioned as extremists who went too far in their quest for equality, becoming like men, giving up their natural roles as mothers, so now they are unhappy (p. 120)—a cautionary "be careful what you wish for" tale for women. There is hope, however, since "we have emerged from the dark, angry nights of early women's liberation into the bright dawn of a Postfeminist era" (Walters, 1995, p. 120). In the new postfeminist narrative, women can reclaim some of the former roles they gave up in the name of feminism and resign their anger and indignation about gender inequalities—relics of an outdated form of feminism. In so doing, women are active and empowered because they are making decisive choices about how to live their lives.

Work/Family Tension Gone

The women in the BI display all the behavior valorized in postfeminist discourse: femininity, heterosexually attractive bodily behavior, desire for marriage and children, and reveling in the male gaze. Surprisingly, however, they are not shown actively choosing this behavior. They do not appear to perform their femininity in a self-conscious manner as an act of protest against feminism, to prove their autonomy, exercise choice, or reclaim a part of their selves to fight outdated and harmful feminist ideals—as we see in postfeminism. The BI women seem to land on the show already having reached these postfeminist goals. The women who win a spot at the rose ceremony on *The Bachelor* have proven their postfeminist mettle. The BI is not a place where postfeminist issues are played out; rather, it is a place where these have been resolved. The type of femininity prescribed by postfeminist discourse is a precondition to entering the competition to find a man in the BI rather than something actively pursued to prove one's postfeminist womanliness (to prove one is not aligned with feminist values). The BI affords a space where sticky postfeminist concerns have already been settled, and women can take the next step in achieving their postfeminist goals: finding a husband.

One of the tensions in postfeminist discourse that does not plague the women in the BI is that "among work, family, and dating/sexuality," (Projansky, 2001, p. 79). As Probyn (1997) suggests, postfeminism articulates choiceoisie as "the possibility of choosing between the home or the career, the family or the successful job" (p. 131). Postfeminism advocates for only one right choice: family and motherhood. In the BI there is no suggestion, as there is in postfeminist discourse, that having a career is the reason why these women are not yet married (Dow, 1996; Walters, 1995), and that they therefore made the wrong choices up until this point. It is evident, from the tag lines (name, age, hometown and occupation) that appear below a participant's name onscreen, that most of the women are college-educated, or in college, and have, or are training for, a career or a respectable professional or middle-class job (doctor, lawyer, contractor, schoolteacher, to name a few). The lowest level jobs are generally as administrative assistants, nannies, flight attendants, and occasionally waitresses (one woman was a homemaker on season fourteen, the only one in all the seasons)—but women with these jobs are few. An implicit requirement for women in the BI is that they be middle-class and educated, and have, or be on their way to having, careers. These are women who have largely resolved the career question—they have the ability to have one—and are now ready to move on to the important task of finding a husband. The postfeminist tension between career and family seems obliterated. Indeed, having a career (or the imminent possibility of one) seems naturally to lead to marriage (and implicitly children) in the BI, rather than present an obstacle in the quest to have it all.

While it may seem that a BI woman's most empowering asset is her career or promising professional future (affording financial security and independence), the series shows the women's desire for a career as secondary to her desire for a husband.[5] Despite making a woman's professional success a necessary prerequisite for the series, alongside a wish to be married, the question of how the women will negotiate career and marriage, and eventually children, is never addressed in any depth. Finding a husband is always the primary focus, the career or potential for a career a precondition. When possible conflict between career and marriage is addressed, it is quickly dealt with, suggesting it is not a serious issue. For instance, when the question arises in *The Bachelor* about whether a woman is willing to move to another city to be with the bachelor, the woman is almost always presented as willing to do so. It is inevitably assumed the woman will move to where the bachelor is and will have no trouble picking up her career in this new location. For instance, school psychologist Helene (the final woman selected by bachelor Aaron in season two) tells Aaron on episode six that she can practice her job anywhere, reassuring him that she is willing to move to be with him. Part of what she likes about her career, she tells the bachelor, is the flexibility of her schedule. She can be there when her children get home from school. Aaron asks Helene if she would like to stay at home while the kids are young, and she responds that she thinks she would.[6] There is no discussion of how staying at home might affect Helene's career or the couple's finances.

Moving to be with the bachelor is an implicit requirement in season thirteen of *The Bachelor*, since starring bachelor Jason has a son. Discussion of the women's willingness to move to Seattle to be with Jason and his son is an ongoing theme. All the women polled are willing to move, and many openly profess their desire to do so. Upon being eliminated on episode three of this season, for instance, Kari tells the camera that she was ready to move to Seattle, be a stepmom to Jason's son, have a family and love Jason, and that she is sad she won't have the opportunity to do all this. When asked by Jason's mother if moving will be a problem for her, Molly from this same season (the woman Jason marries), who is presented as very career-minded, says it will not be a problem since she can have her career in Seattle and still have a family alongside her career. In fact, Molly talks about how she has spent the last few years focusing on her career but is now looking for something deeper. She is ready for the next step, she says, which is to settle down by getting married and having children. Marriage is thus the logical next step after securing, though perhaps not maintaining, a career.

On *The Bachelorette*, however, it is another story. Though it was assumed the men on the first season of *The Bachelorette* would move to Los Angeles to be with bachelorette Trista, Ryan, a fireman and Trista's chosen man, was reluctant to move. During the visit to his hometown on episode four, Ryan says he does not want to move from his home in Vail, Colorado, since it would mean leaving his fire station and family. In his words, it would be like "giving up a part of myself." Predictably, Trista and Ryan bought a house in Vail and moved there after their wedding. This question emerges again on season five of *The Bachelorette* with bachelorette Jillian. When one bachelor expresses concern about having to move to her hometown, Vancouver, she quickly says that although she is a "career girl" she wants to "put herself in someone else's hands for a while" and does not want her chosen guy to move to Vancouver. At the same time, Jillian's career is a constant on this season, with Jillian repeatedly mentioning how much she has given up (in terms of her career) to be on the series. In other words, career is important to Jillian, but love is more important and career will easily take a backseat once she finds love. In the "After the Final Rose" episode of season six of *The Bachelorette*, we learn that Ali and Roberto (Ali's final man) relocate together to San Diego (Roberto lives in Charleston, SC, Ali in San Francisco). In other words, both relocate but Roberto does not move specifically to where Ali lives.

Ali, star of the sixth season of *The Bachelorette* and a participant on season fourteen of *The Bachelor*, expressly deals with the conflict between the demands of her career as an advertising account manager and those of finding love (the demands of the BI stand in for love in this context). She is the only woman in the BI who tackles these issues explicitly.[7] On episode six of *The Bachelor*, Ali tearfully tells bachelor Jake that she got a call from work telling her she has to return to work immediately or lose her job. She agonizes over her decision, but ultimately leaves the show. Of course, she regrets her decision and asks Jake if she can return (he refuses). In "The Women Tell All" episode, Ali talks about how she made the wrong choice, that one should not choose work over love, adding that she will never make the same mistake again. The BI has faith in her assertions, it seems, since it offers her the opportunity to star in season six of *The Bachelorette*. On *The Bachelorette*, she repeatedly affirms that she learned her lesson about choosing work over love and that she is now ready to risk everything to find love (taking the necessary risk to find love thus also involves prioritizing love over career). While she continues to talk about the importance of her career, we are led to believe that the conflict between appearing on the series and maintaining her career (ultimately between having a husband and having a career) will never again be an issue, because she has learned the hard way that love must always trump career. This experience enables Ali to affirm that she now has her priorities straight and is therefore ready to find love.

Ali is the perfect postfeminist poster-girl: choose love and husband over career, always. However, she exemplifies a twist to this setup, one integral for the women in the BI. While she has a desire for career and the ability to create a solid career for herself, she prioritizes love—but this, only after she has established her ability to maintain a career. This is slightly different from postfeminist discourse, since she does not forgo career for love; rather, she must have a career in place before searching for love. Once her priorities are in order, the conflict between career and love is fairly easily resolved, with absolutely no details given about her work situation or any discussion of how she may be jeopardizing her career by being on the series. In other words, it appears as if her career conflicts are magically resolved once she makes the right decision. She still has a career and plans to return to it once the series is over, but not to the detriment of finding love and getting married. In this way, career is always already there for Ali if she desires it, which seems to be the case for most of the women in the BI.

A Man, Any Man

The most stressful aspect of marriage for the women in the BI is finding a husband (and in Ali's case, committing to finding a husband—making this her priority). Once this mission is accomplished, the fairy tale is complete. Indeed, the women's comments when first introduced on *The Bachelor* clearly indicate that marriage is either the final piece that will complete the women's lives or the fulfillment of a lifelong dream. For instance, twenty-four-year-old interior designer Erin tells us in season two, "I've done all the things I've wanted to do. I've settled in my career, I have all my friends, I'm ready to meet someone I care about and who cares about me and start our new life together." Twenty-six-year-old attorney Darla tells us in season four, "I feel pretty fulfilled with everything in terms of me personally and professionally, except for the fact that I don't have love. I haven't met the right guy." Many of the women describe a lifelong fantasy of getting married. General contractor Tara, twenty-three years old and the second runner-up for the bachelor's affection in season five, tells the cameras, "since I was really young, I've always been planning my wedding. My mom actually made me this tiny little wedding dress when I was young. I think my friends and I married just about everybody who came over to play." Some of the images introducing the women to viewers show them trying on wedding gowns (before they ever meet the bachelor). Shannon, a twenty-six-year-old human resources director from season three, is shown trying on gowns as she describes in detail in voice-over, how she imagines her wedding day. Liz, a twenty-three-year-old event marketing director from season three, tries on her mother's wedding gown for the camera as she tells her mother she hopes she gets to wear it for the bachelor. Elizabeth, also from season three, a twenty-four-year-old child life specialist, tells the camera tearfully as she sits on the arm of the chair in which her dad sits, "all I want, all I want is for my dad to walk me down the aisle and see me go off and get married . . . just walk me down the aisle of a church, even if I don't get married, and I don't get the opportunity, just walk me, in a white dress." Devastated when eliminated on the first episode of season thirteen of *The Bachelor* after just meeting Jason, Jackie tells the camera she had already fully planned her wedding to Jason in her head, thinking she had found the man of her dreams.

As for the women who star in the six seasons of *The Bachelorette*, they are specifically ready to find a husband, not to meet a particular type of man (other than one they can marry). About the first three bachelorettes, Trista, Meredith, and Jen, Chris reassures us in the first episode of the season that they are not only beautiful but accomplished, and not just accomplished but ready to marry—suggesting that while being accomplished might be impressive, when combined with a desire for marriage, then a woman is *really* special. On the first episode of the first season of *The Bachelorette*, Chris says that Trista is "gorgeous, sexy, a Miami Heat dancer," but that "there's a lot you don't know about the beautiful twenty-nine-year-old blond." She's "a highly educated career woman" who has "dedicated her career to working with children as a pediatric physical therapist." Then Trista says she wants "to find Mr. Right. I want to find him . . . and I've dreamt about my wedding for a long time." On the first episode of the second season of *The Bachelorette*, Chris tells us that Meredith has a "degree in fine arts, launched a dual career as a makeup artist and model," and now "she's pursuing a lifelong dream of attending culinary school and looking forward to sharing a bright future with the man of her dreams." On the first episode of the third season of *The Bachelorette*, Chris says of Jen that "she's beautiful, she's sexy" and that after getting her bachelor's degree in business, "she's focusing on her new career as an events coordinator." He adds, "and now she's ready to take a second chance on love." Then Jen tells us "I want to get married, and I want to have a family, and I want to stop searching, and I want to settle down." In season four, however, the series forgoes the career thing entirely: there's nary a mention of what Deanna does for a living (the bio for Deanna on the ABC website tells us she's a real estate agent). On the first episode of the season, Chris tells us she is a "woman who has already won America's heart," and Deanna asserts confidently to the camera, "I expect to find my husband at the end of this." The focus is on her desire to find a man, and her worth is her ability to capture the hearts of all the men who are there specifically to meet her (and of all of America). Jillian, star of season five of *The Bachelorette*, is a successful interior designer, as we are told repeatedly throughout the season. When she talks with Chris about what she's hoping will happen on the show, she tells Chris her favorite saying: "you have to slay a few dragons to find the right prince." While the saying suggests a reversal of gender roles, with the woman taking on the conventional role of the man who fights danger and scary creatures on his quest to find his princess (perhaps an empowering fantasy), it is quickly apparent that the desire is for a man who will play the role of husband rather than for a specific man with particular qualities. Jillian tells Chris that at the end of slaying all her dragons she's going to find her "mister invisible" and unveil him, since she doesn't know what he looks like yet. Then she recounts that her mother told her to "just bring us a great prince charming, . . . cuz I'm ready to have grandchildren." Jillian is looking for a husband and a father for her children, not a particular kind of man. Ali, star of season six of *The Bachelorette*, affirms her desire for a husband in the first episode by stating that she has learned her lesson about making the mistake of putting "desk and computer and keyboard over someone who could be the love of my life." She tells Chris that it has been hard for her to make love and a relationship a priority, that in the past she let her insecurities and fears dictate her life, but that she is not going to be a victim to this anymore. She affirms she's ready to get on with her life, "to meet someone and ... to put them first." Having lost out with Jake, the man she fell in love with on season fourteen of *The Bachelorette*, Ali is now ready to find his replacement.

Of course, this attitude toward marriage is gender-specific: the men are rarely shown talking in any detail about their desire for marriage specifically. In fact, bachelor Bob from season four of *The Bachelor* writes in his autobiography that he "was scared when he was offered the starring role in *The Bachelor*. It seemed as if there would be so much pressure on me to propose to one of the women at the end. Even though I've had time to heal from my divorce, I didn't know when—if ever—I would be ready to commit to marrying someone again" (Guiney, 2003, p. 151). In other words, he starred in the series without a burning desire for marriage, a vital requirement for all the women in the BI. Perhaps the men's feelings on marriage are best summed up by Chris on the first episode of the first season of *The Bachelorette*: "now granted, you usually don't hear of men lining up to get married, but these men are here because of their romantic feelings for Trista, each of them hoping they might be the last man standing and that Trista will be their wife."[8] Indeed, Jeremy, one of the men on *The Bachelorette* season four says, "I'm going on the show for Deanna quite simply. Deanna is a combination of personality and looks, and it just doesn't exist. For me, Deanna is my unicorn." In other words, the women are so special that the men will consider marrying them. In essence, as Chris comments on the first episode of season three of *The Bachelorette*: "the men are coming here tonight for more than just the promise of finding true love. They are here for the woman herself, Jen Schefft." The men are not looking specifically for marriage but if they meet the right woman, they will consider it. The series shows the women, on the other hand, wanting marriage even before they meet their prospective husband (many dreaming of marriage since they were a child) and paying far less attention to which man they will marry: what matters is finding *a* man.

Empowerment Without Choice

In many ways the BI shows are a perfect example of what Probyn (1993) says about choosing marriage and children in postfeminist discourse: it is "naturally every woman's choice" (p. 278). Choosing marriage and children is presented as the right choice to make over other choices. However, in the BI, there is very little choice. Instead, women are offered the much-desired endpoint of a series of successfully completed tasks that ideally lead to marriage. The potential for marriage is the reward for tasks done well, a foregone conclusion. Here the journey for the women diverges from that outlined by Probyn when it comes to choiceosie, because they do not explicitly make any choices.

Though empowerment through choice is much vaunted in the BI, consistent with postfeminist discourse, the choices to which the women have access are even more limited than the choices privileged in postfeminist discourse. The BI host is quick to point out that the women have power, as mentioned earlier ("you are completely empowered here"), though only after telling them bachelor Bob will be making the crucial decisions (about whether they can stay). When all is said and done, the empowered choices a woman has are few: she can decide to stay only if the bachelor offers her this choice, or she can reject the bachelor's invitation to stay. The only choice she can make that is not dependent on the bachelor's choice is to leave before he makes his decision.

As the season progresses, even this small range of choice narrows. This is reflected in the use of the word "empowered," which Chris employs frequently in his first few statements, usually in his statement at the first rose ceremony, and then sometimes in later ceremonies and later seasons. However, Chris makes less frequent speeches as the seasons progress, and when he does make a speech in the later seasons, he no longer uses the word "empowered." The older *The Bachelor* series becomes, and presumably the more familiar audiences and participants are with its format, the less the series reminds women that they are empowered, suggesting the women already know the ropes at this stage (having watched previous seasons), or that it is no longer relevant enough to be worth mentioning. What is notable is that on none of the seasons of *The Bachelorette* does Chris tell the men that they are "empowered," emphasizing the gender specificity of the term.

The idea of women making choices is forefronted in season six of *The Bachelor*, where the format of the first show differs from that of other seasons: it begins with two potential bachelors (usually by the first episode one is already selected by producers), and at the end of the first hour of the two-hour episode, the women vote for one or the other of the bachelors. Chris introduces the first episode by telling viewers that "the women are truly empowered" since "they will decide who will stay and who will go." Once the women have made this initial choice, however, there are no more empowering choices to be made. In addition, their initial choice puts the women who voted for the losing bachelor in jeopardy, because the other women saw the voting process and can tell the winning bachelor which women voted against him, even though the bachelor himself does not get to see who votes for whom.

What is most interesting about the seasons in which Chris makes speeches using the word "empowered" is how his comments change around the third rose ceremony, when the word "empowered" begins to disappear from his vocabulary. At this point he comments instead on the mounting difficulties of the process and the developing feelings of everyone involved, suggesting that the intensity of the experience and the feelings are now what rule participants, supplanting their access to empowered choices. The further along the women make it in a season, the more emotions and feelings enter into the picture and the less the series frames their choices as empowering: the women seem to lose their agency in the face of this overpowering experience. For example, when bachelor Bob has to narrow the pool from three to two women in season four, Chris says to the women that he understands each of them is "in love with Bob," and then he wishes them luck—no mention of being "empowered" as in earlier speeches. Feelings, emotions, and ultimately falling in love, deprive the women of choice or empowerment; all they are left with is luck.

One of Chris's speeches is particularly poignant because of the alignment of the women's limited access to empowered choices with their seemingly increased feelings for the bachelor. At the sixth rose ceremony in season three, Chris says to the women:

> Ladies, good evening. I just talked to Andrew. This decision is going to be incredibly tough on him. I can only imagine it's going to be equally tough on the three of you . . . Now this is where I usually tell you that you are all totally empowered here, and you are, but after talking to Andrew tonight, and looking in your eyes and feeling the tension in this room right now, I think we all realize just how serious this has become.

A connection is explicitly drawn between empowerment and mounting feelings. Chris notes that it is his habit to tell the women "you are all totally empowered here," and he reassures them that they are. However, there is a "but" to this empowerment, followed by a comment about looking into the women's eyes and feeling the tension in the room, suggesting that their empowerment is mediated by the emotion and feelings involved in the experience of getting closer to the bachelor. While Chris does not go so far as to tell the women that they are no longer empowered, he does tell them that the situation has become serious, suggesting that the more serious the situation (the more their feelings are involved), the less the women are empowered. Hence, while participants still have choices, they are less likely to exercise them because of the feelings they develop for the bachelor. The stronger their feelings, the more likely they are to transfer power to the bachelor (who will make the important choices). Falling in love, the series' aim, is ultimately disempowering. Indeed, feeling love makes empowerment a moot point: who would choose empowerment when they can have love (similarly, who would choose work when they can have love, as suggested by the way Ali's situation with her work is framed)? I am not claiming empowerment and love are in opposition but rather that empowerment becomes unnecessary once love enters the picture. Empowerment and career are pastimes the women engage in until they find love, their final goal. After that, they may still be empowered, and they may still have a career, but what is most important is that they have a man.

In the BI, women do not choose to fall in love. They fall in love and as such are at the mercy of what the object of their affection decides to do with that love. The BI moves beyond choiceoisie to a space where women no longer need worry about making *any* choices; rather, they worry about finishing a challenging obstacle course that, if completed successfully, leads to marriage and a family. The space the BI creates for women cannot be fully articulated through postfeminist discourse. While the women behave in ways that fit with the imperatives of postfeminist discourse, they move away from the central issues of this discourse.

No Empowerment for the Men

Most revealing perhaps is the absence of the word "empowerment" from all six seasons of *The Bachelorette*, though Chris does tell the men during some of the introductory speeches to the rose ceremony that "they always have a say." Empowerment is an idea reserved for the women. In fact, the gendering of love and empowerment in the BI is salient in some of the speeches Chris makes to the men on *The Bachelorette*. Here's a sampling of some of these speeches: At the third rose ceremony of season one, Chris says to the men, "I can only imagine how difficult this process has been for you guys. Maybe a little awkward the way the tables have been turned. So, we want to thank you for your openness and willingness to try and find true love this way." At the fourth rose ceremony he says, "I know you've all developed feelings for Trista, but unfortunately Trista can only repay the favor to three of you." At the fifth rose ceremony, Chris says, "tonight is going to be incredibly tough on her. I can only imagine it's gonna be equally difficult for each of you. Let's be honest. I think we'd all agree things have changed. It's fair to say all three of you have deep feelings for Trista." In season two, on the third episode, Chris says, "fellows, honestly, for the first time, I don't know what's gonna happen. Meredith is unbelievably torn. She's supposed to come down here and hand out six boutonnière roses tonight. She just told me she might need a seventh rose." At the sixth rose ceremony during the same season, Chris says, "I think it goes without saying she has an incredibly tough decision to make tonight. You stand before me having just returned from three very special overnight dates." In these speeches in season five, Chris talks about how difficult the process has been for Jillian, and on episode eight Chris comments that the men have flown halfway around the world for Jillian (this season has the show set in different countries almost every week). Note that there is never any mention of love in these comments—deep feelings, but no love (though there is talk of the men's attempts to find love). In fact, the men's feelings for Trista on season one are to be repaid as a "favor": she owes them for their affection for her. In season five, Chris highlights the lengths to which the men have gone (flying around the world) to be with Jillian. In seasons two and five, Chris's speeches focus on Meredith's and Jillian's feelings and on the difficulties involved for them in this process, not on how the men feel. In essence, the men are commended for sticking it out for so long in an uncomfortable situation, while the women are congratulated on making it this far.

The women are in a more vulnerable position in this setup, since the more emotionally involved they become, the less empowered they are. Given the importance of the proper display of emotion, outlined in Chapters 3 and 4, the danger of this setup for the women is apparent: for the women, agreeing to the process is not just a question of choice, as it is for the men, but rather of a choice that will supposedly empower them. Moreover, implicitly, the women should feel lucky to be given the opportunity to be with a man. Indeed, at every commercial break before most rose ceremonies on *The Bachelor*, the host tells viewers to stay tuned to find out "who will go home broken-hearted," while on *The Bachelorette* he entreats the audience to stay tuned to find out "who will have his ego shattered." The choice of words reveals what is at stake and what the risks of falling in love are for each gender: for the women the process involves the heart, for the men the ego.[9]

Moving in and out of Postfeminism

Other than an education and a career (or a pending career), the "exceptional" qualities of the women (as per the selection criteria) are decidedly antifeminist according to even the broadest definition of feminism: achievement of a mainstream standard of beauty; inviting the male gaze; willingness to compete with other women for a man; privileging finding a husband and having a family over all else. This combination of requirements suggests the BI is a postfeminist text, that is, a continuation of the trend in television to show women struggling to "have it all" (career, family, children, femininity, the male gaze) that includes postfeminist shows such as *Ally McBeal* (Dubrofsky, 2002; Kim, 2001; Moseley and Read, 2002; Newman, 2000; Ouellette, 2002;) and *Sex and the City* (Arthurs, 2003; Kim, 2001; Owen, Stein and Vande Berg, 2007). However, though the BI texts rely on postfeminist tropes and affirm postfeminist desires, they do away with important tensions in postfeminist discourse.[10] The BI moves in and out of postfeminist discourse, and it is this slippage that is of interest.

As mentioned earlier, the BI presents a world where women can realize their postfeminist desires in an uncomplicated and unconflicted manner. The women arrive already fitting a mainstream heterosexual standard of beauty without actively choosing it, without a fight against an outdated notion of feminism that would have them give up such popularly constructed essential feminine qualities. Further, a career is a precondition for access to finding a husband in the BI not an obstacle to be overcome by making the right choice (to get married and have a family). Unlike in postfeminist media texts, women's desires do no conflict in the BI; they coexist amiably. Indeed, the man who lands a woman from the BI is very lucky: he has found a woman who is ambitious, educated, independent, but willing to give it all up (if need be) to marry him.

I am not suggesting life is easy for the women in the BI. Clearly they work hard to be and remain on the series (by setting themselves up for a career, achieving a certain appearance, and engaging in heterosexually attractive bodily behavior) so they can have the opportunity to meet the man of their dreams and fulfill their postfeminist desires. However, it is still true that for these women there are no tough decisions, no tough choices, no self-conscious activist behavior—only hard work. The task is different for women in postfeminist discourse: make the right choice (choose family over work) or end up an ambitious career woman out of touch with her essential womanhood, a lonely lost soul (Walters, 1995, p. 121). In the BI, on the other hand, all choices are ultimately reconciled, one desire leading to access to the next. There are no difficult or even right or wrong choices. There are simply no choices. Or rather, in the BI the biggest choice is the decision to open up and take the risk necessary for finding love. Once this is done, the rest falls into place.

The BI shows women trying to reach postfeminist goals oblivious to the painful realities of female oppression—realities that are, to some extent, still apparent in postfeminist discourse for a certain demographic of women (white, heterosexual, middle-class). How are we to understand this world of the BI, where women need not fight against injustice, where gender inequality does not exist, where the plight of women globally or even nationally is irrelevant and all is subservient to women finding a mate? Feminist television scholars need to extend scholarship on postfeminist discourse to account for television texts such as the BI shows that take up the goals of postfeminism but do away with postfeminist obstacles and tensions.

In trying to understand the space of the BI, I use the term "postfeminist nirvana," a term first coined by Goodstein in 1992 to describe a state where women have the best of both worlds, home and work. I extend this definition. In the BI, there is a utopic postfeminist space where women exist. This is the "postfeminist nirvana," a peaceful, unconflicted state one strives to attain but never quite reaches. The term "postfeminist nirvana" pushes the boundaries of scholarship on postfeminism, suggesting there is a new breed of representations of women on television, one that harkens back to the 1950s images of the good housewife (June Cleaver) and the sexy blonde bombshell (Marilyn Monroe), rolling these into one package. The term also takes into account the advances women have made in the workforce since the 1950s. The woman who lives in the "postfeminist nirvana" no longer has to deal with the postfeminist complications of navigating tensions between career and family, maintaining attractiveness and so forth. These tensions vanish, since women are led by strong emotions and desires (and willing to be led by these since they are necessary to finding love) that make choice irrelevant.

While the women may be in a state of postfeminist nirvana during their journey on the BI, most never reach "nirvana" in the end, since what they are ultimately trying to achieve, marriage, is constantly just out of their reach—always sought after, but never attained. For indeed, at the time of this writing only two of the women from the BI, Trista (a participant on the first season of *The Bachelor* and the star of the first season of *The Bachelorette*), and Molly (from season thirteen of *The Bachelor*) actually land husbands out of the process.

When the host congratulates the women in the speech quoted earlier, he is implicitly congratulating them on having reached a state of "postfeminist nirvana," a state that prepares them for a happy union with the "man of their dreams." The BI moves us beyond notions of empowerment and choice, and in their place we are given overwhelming feelings and emotions, guiding forces that supplant even the limited choices offered by postfeminist discourse.

Notes

1.   In some seasons, we see professionals on hand to do hair and makeup for the women for the first and the final rose ceremonies, but it is not clear if this is the case for every season or for every rose ceremony.

2.   During the first episode of some seasons of *The Bachelor*, details are given about how the women were selected.

3.   In the first episodes of seasons two and three, we are told that the twenty-five finalists beat out eleven thousand women for a spot on the series.

4.   After appearing on the series, the men are more likely to meet more of these types of women thanks to their newfound celebrity status. For instance, Bob, star of the fourth season of *The Bachelor*, met and married soap opera starlet Rebecca Budig (*All My Children*) when both were filming *Bachelor XYZ*, an ABC Family recap of highlights from *The Bachelor*.

5.   Feminist concerns arise indirectly in the second season of *The Bachelorette* when Lanny brings Meredith home to meet his family. The series gives a lot of time to a scene in which Lanny's mother tells Meredith that her role as Lanny's wife will be to honor, respect, and obey him. She tells Meredith that in terms of priorities, God comes first, husband second, and job third. When laid out this way, Meredith balks: during this scene, we see shots of Meredith's face, looking very uncomfortable, and then we see Meredith say in private to the camera that Lanny's mother was very intense and protective and that the meeting was difficult for her. Lanny does not receive a rose at the end of this episode. As with Summer, the series codes Lanny's mother as odd. In this instance, the coding works to verify Meredith as a progressive, independent, and empowered woman, unlike Lanny's mother. Nonetheless, the action in the BI upholds the prioritizing of husband over work, as Lanny's mother insists is necessary.

6.   There are the rare women, such as twenty-one-year-old student Jessica K. on season five of *The Bachelor* who admits in the first episode that she wants to be a mother and wife primarily: "I think I would rather find someone that is a provider for the family . . . I wouldn't mind, like, part-time working . . . I do want to raise a family and I want to be, like, well-off so money is not an issue."

7.   Ed, the final man Jillian selects on season five of *The Bachelorette*, faces a

similar situation when his work informs him, while he is on the show, that he has to return to work if he wants to keep his job. He agonizes over his decision and decides to leave the show and return to work. On the next episode, viewers see him regretting his decision and asking Jillian to take him back. She does. Other than affirmations by Ed that he made the wrong choice to return to work, there is no more discussion about his career. There seems to be an implicit assumption that work will not be an issue. This conflict between career and love is but a blip on his quest to ultimately finding love.

8.　In the six seasons of *The Bachelorette*, the starring women's identities were known before the men applied to be on the series. In other words, the men apply specifically to meet these women not necessarily because they desire marriage. For many seasons of *The Bachelor* this is not the case. The women do not know who the bachelor is prior to applying to be on the show.

9.　Mirroring the traditional Western body (female) vs. mind (male) dialectic.

10.　I am grateful to Sarah Projansky for pointing this out and helping me develop my thinking on this point.

Conclusion: The "Ideal" Woman?

What are we to take away from the ideas produced by the BI? The BI raises a bunch of questions about reality, authenticity, surveillance, and gender. While Andrejevic (2004) explores the "work of being watched" in his scholarship on reality TV, we might ask: what is the work of watching others being watched? The BI's "frenzy of the visible" (Williams, 1989) makes sure viewers see participants experiencing real emotion (even if decontextualized): we see them cry, we see them rage. How does the notion of accessing a kind of real or authentic in reality television (no matter how constructed this may be) give a certain tenor to reality shows not present, for instance, in scripted shows? Ouellette (2004) suggests, in her work on the television series *Judge Judy*, that the show teaches lower-income women the lessons of neo-liberalism: how to take care of yourself and how to be a responsible citizen. Similarly, we might ask of reality television, as Hay (2003), and Hay and Ouellette (2008) ask, in what ways can television be seen as part of the neo-liberalization of the domestic sphere[1]? How might the BI teach viewers how to be a romantic partner? What does it suggest is the work of the good citizen in the process of finding love? In what ways can the BI texts be read as a manual for how to be an ideal romantic partner, or as a description of what *not* to do in the process of looking for love?

Women on the Losing End

Ironically, while women are the stars in the BI, more women than men are on the losing end of the game quantitatively: Trista, Meredith, Jen, Deanna, Jillian, and Ali, stars of *The Bachelorette*, reject approximately one hundred and fifty men in total, while Alex, Aaron, Andrew, Bob, Jesse, Byron, Charlie, Travis

Stork, Lorenzo, Andy, Brad Womack, Matt, Jason, and Jake, stars of *The Bachelor*, reject around three hundred and forty women total. Statistically, more women than men suffer in the process of finding love in each series of the BI (as well, most couples break up shortly after the finale).

As mentioned, though the gender positions are reversed in *The Bachelorette*, the gender expectations and roles remain the same as in *The Bachelor*. While it might seem that the scenario of *The Bachelor*, with one man choosing from twenty-five women, places women in one of the least empowering positions imaginable, and that conversely placing one woman on *The Bachelorette* in the position of selecting one man from among twenty-five is a more empowering scenario for a woman, this is not the case. Switching the genders of the central player does not change the balance of power: the ways women are to gain power and their means of access to this power in *The Bachelorette* are consistent with how these play out in *The Bachelor*, affording women little power in the space of the BI

Thus far, the BI has produced fourteen seasons of *The Bachelor*, only six seasons of *The Bachelorette*. The numbers are telling. For instance, *The Bachelor* pulled in $38.2 million in profit for the sixth season in contrast to *The Bachelorette*'s $27.7 million for the second season (Patsuris, September 7, 2004). Thirty-second advertising spots on *The Bachelor* go for $53,400 more than those for *The Bachelorette* (Patsuris, September 7, 2004). *The Bachelor* is overall more successful than *The Bachelorette*. The shortcomings of *The Bachelorette* (as an entertaining series, as a consistent ratings success compared to *The Bachelor*) highlight the imperatives upon which *The Bachelor* relies. A series that centers on women providing the dramatic action does not work well if there is only one woman on display, especially if this one woman is constructed as an ideal woman (as she is on *The Bachelorette*). The BI may purport to be about helping two people find love, but the bulk of the action is about women who fail at love, of which there are plenty on *The Bachelor* and none on *The Bachelorette*.

In the end, most of the women in the BI are not ideal for love, since all but one of the original pool of twenty-five are eliminated. There are, of course, degrees of "goodness" and "badness," and some of the women eliminated are not specifically marked as "bad." However, the women who occupy center stage are generally the "bad" women. This begs the question: what kind of ideal woman does the BI produce in those rare moments when she appears? What does this creature look like?

The finalists in each season of *The Bachelor*, Amanda from season one, Helene from season two, Estella Gardinier from season three, Jen from season four, Jessica Bowlin from season five, Mary from season six, Sarah Brice from season seven, Sarah Stone from season eight, Jennifer Wilson from season nine, Tessa from season ten, Shayne Lamas from season twelve, Melissa from season thirteen (though Jason dumps her for Molly on the "After the Final Rose Part I" episode), are all, to some extent, "ideal" women. There is one notable exception,

Vienna Girardi, bachelor Jake's final woman on season fourteen. Vienna is perhaps the exception that illustrates the convention. She is the only final woman who is center stage throughout her season and disliked by almost everyone. Much of the episode when Jake brings Vienna home to meet his family focuses on how long it takes for his family to be won over by her, with emphasis on the moments when she offends family members with her behavior. Ultimately, even the bachelor dislikes her, evident in their explosive breakup, featured at the end of the seventh episode of season six of *The Bachelorette* when the now estranged couple is interviewed together (not separately as were Helene and Aaron from season two, perhaps to ensure fireworks). On this episode they call each other names, get angry, and Vienna finally storms off.

Up until the very end of other seasons of *The Bachelor*, the focus is generally on the women who are not chosen as the final woman, not on the final woman (though inordinate attention is paid to Shayne in season twelve, where the focus is on trying to determine her sincerity in the process—whether she is after love or fame). During the finale of season five of *The Bachelor*, for instance, much screen time is given to Tara, the second runner-up. Viewers see her becoming anxious and nervous about the bachelor's final decision and watch her get physically ill (she throws up) during the limousine ride to see the bachelor. She asks both the host and the bachelor to give her a moment to collect herself before moving on with the proceedings. There is very little focus on the winner, Jessica. In fact, some of Jessica's time onscreen is devoted to her watching (from a window above the garden where the final ceremony takes place) as the bachelor explains to Tara that he is in love with another woman. Jessica may be the winner, but Tara is the star of this episode.

Even the women selected by the men in the finales, who are seemingly ideal for love, do not stand the test of time. Their relationships with the bachelor fall apart, and they do not win the ultimate postfeminist prize: love, marriage, and a family. All in all, in postfeminist terms the BI has produced only two women ideal for love: Trista, who appeared in the first season of *The Bachelor*, subsequently starred in the first season of *The Bachelorette* and married her chosen man; and Molly from season thirteen of *The Bachelor*, who eventually married bachelor Jake (though she was originally rejected by him in the finale).

Expert Women

Postfeminist prize or not, to do well on the BI a woman must be expert at all things stereotypically considered feminine: expressing emotions, confessing, connecting, and therapeutizing (Chodorow, 1978; DeFranciso, Leto and O'Connor, 1995; Gilligan, 1982; Hare-Mustin, 1997; Simonds, 1992, 1996). This means that the status of a woman in the BI is instantly at risk if she does not show expertise in these areas: she fails at love and fails as a woman, since she is unable to show proficiency at the skills that will prove her feminine allure. In some ways, the story I tell about women in the BI is a very old one: women are rigidly disciplined and constrained by gender expectations, they must be relationship experts, they must express emotion in a specific way, and they are visually objectified. However, what is new is that the task of finding love in the BI is always intertwined with one's seeming attitude toward surveillance. This story also incorporates contemporary tropes about postfeminism, therapeutic discourse, and race.

Chapter 1 looked at the need for women to authenticate themselves under surveillance, and the alignment of whiteness with naturalness. In these ways, a woman in the BI needs to act, while under surveillance and being observed by a crew, the way it is imagined she behaves when not in this situation.

Chapter 2 looked at the representation of women of color in *The Bachelor*. While women of color do not signify within the romantic paradigms of the series (as potential suitors), they must nonetheless play along, pretending to be oblivious to the ways in which they are used to inspire white people to find love. If she is lucky, a woman of color might be able to help one of the white women show who she really is. The ideal white woman, on the other hand, learns that the "foreign," the "exotic," is not only sexy and romantic but that overcoming its potential dangers can be one of the surest ways to test true love. Further, the ideal woman does not balk at the prospect of her man sharing intimacies with other women, confident as she is in the knowledge that if her man really loves her, his sexual dilettantism will only increase his desire (and eventually his ability) to be monogamous with her. She must accept that she is living in a harem and at the same time pretend she is in a monogamous relationship with one man.

Chapters 3 and 4 outlined the prescribed emotional economy on the series and the affiliation between emotional displays and a woman's ability to take the necessary risk to find love. Putting together the requirements here, the ideal woman should be emotional and show she is ready for love. She must not balk at the fact of surveillance or the contrived setting, always ready to say how she feels and make herself emotionally vulnerable for a man. However, she better be careful not to appear too emotional. While she should express strong feelings for her man, she should not express these too strongly or too soon. She must show her feelings in an emotional way and confess these to the appropriate people, but she must be careful not to say the wrong thing to the wrong person or express her feelings too strongly too soon (to anyone). Not only must she be in control of herself at all times (though not afraid of losing control of her emotions enough to show that she is willing to find love), she must also be careful that her emotions do not betray her. She needs to be especially mindful to ensure that her emotions only serve to reaffirm the image she originally presented of herself. Importantly, her behavior must be consistent and never a surprise. Finally, while ultimately she has no control over the situation, since the workers on the series manage the final product, she will nonetheless be judged for her ability to control how she appears in this final, mediated product.

Chapter 5 outlined the "therapeutics of the self," where the self is asserted using paradigms and terms from therapy, implicitly suggesting that the affirmation of an unchanging self somehow accesses the rewards of a therapeutic transformation. Based on the elements in this chapter, the ideal woman in the BI is self-confident. She knows who she is. She is proud of who she is. She can have confidence in herself and in her presentation of self because this has been verified by surveillance—it was caught on film for all to see. She will claim her representation on the series as under her control, despite the fact that it is the result of decisions made by the makers of the show. She will never, *ever* suddenly reveal a different side of herself: she will be exactly who she has always presented herself as being. Getting to know this woman is a continual affirmation that she is exactly who she consistently appeared to be.[2] This is a woman one can count on to never surprise, and her consistency and her pride in this are her two greatest assets.

Chapter 6 argued that the BI creates a space for postfeminist women where they no longer need worry about the tensions of postfeminism, the tensions between work and family. Based on this chapter, the ideal woman for the BI is white and middle-class, has a career, is heterosexual and has the aesthetic appearance of a starlet (and is willing to put the effort into maintaining this appearance). This woman should have a strong desire for a career but need not worry about how to maintain her career, since finding love with a man always seems to clear up any potential conflicts a relationship might pose to her career. Living as she does in a "postfeminist nirvana," she feels empowered by the fact that her life is conflict-free, that she does not have to make any difficult choices, and she gains comfort in the knowledge that as long as she gives her power to the man she loves, her life will progress along a path that will lead to a husband, children, and maybe a career. Most amazingly, this woman will find that the more she lets her feelings develop for her man, the less likely she is to feel the need to make any decisions since her strong feelings and her man will guide her.

Ideal Women for Love?

Drawing together all the requirements of the ideal woman in the BI highlights the complex minefield of paradoxes and contradictions with which a woman trying to find love in the BI must contend: (1) show her emotions and feelings, but not too many too soon; (2) confess her feelings and emotions, but not too much or too soon; (3) show that she is willing to take the risk to find love by overcoming the contrived setting of the series, but not acknowledge the contrived setting; (4) show a comfort with surveillance, but pretend she is not being surveilled; (5) see the process of the series as a therapeutic experience, but not change herself; (6) reveal herself increasingly on the series, but never reveal anything new or startling; (7) be empowered through her choices, but give up power to her emotions and to a man who will make important choices for her; (8) willingly participate in a harem, but eschew the values of the harem; (9) accept that her man is not being monogamous, but make herself available only to him; and (10) claim that her representation on the series is under her control (and claim her pride in this) even though she has little control over this.

Reading through this list of paradoxes highlights the fundamental impossibility of any such creature existing—or at least, the impossibility of her existing and being sane. But, does this really matter in the BI? Many of the most memorable moments are ones with women like Trish, Lee-Ann, Christi, Summer, and even Heather—women who are emotional, defiant, or angry. Perhaps ideal women in the BI are like unicorns. In fact, Jeremy, one of the men on season four of *The Bachelorette* calls star Deanna his unicorn, because he believes her to be a unique combination of good looks and good personality. Sasha echoes this sentiment on season five of *The Bachelorette* when he says, of his attempt to find love, that he is looking for a unicorn that is mythical—rare, beautiful, never actually seen. The action of the series is perhaps about how women can never meet these ideals, about the impossibility of this ideal. Trista, Meredith, Jen, DeAnna, Jillian, and Ali are the closest incarnations: women who never surprise, who are always consistent in their behavior and, I would suggest, who are ultimately quite boring.

This is only true of Jen, however, until the "After The Final Rose" episode. In the live airing of this episode, Jen does surprise. She becomes a woman who fails at love, and spectacularly so at that. On live TV, Jen rejects her suitor Jerry's proposal and gives him the classic "let's just be friends" line. For the rest of this episode, Jen is questioned by everyone (the audience and the host) on her behavior. Her rejected suitor, Jerry, comes to her rescue, telling the audience how wonderful Jen is and that he has no "hard feelings" toward her. Audience members are unconvinced. One woman in the audience asks Jen what it will take to "satisfy" her, insisting that after failing with bachelor Andrew from season three of *The Bachelor* and failing to find a man on *The Bachelorette*, nothing will ever fill her needs. She is not only insatiable but, perhaps frighteningly, voracious as well. In this episode, Jen is cast as unfit for love: she behaves in an incomprehensible, unpredictable manner. Indeed, with this live episode, the third season of *The Bachelorette* accomplishes what every season of *The Bachelor* had done so well (and other seasons of *The Bachelorette* failed to do): expose a woman failing at love, offer the spectacle of a woman failing at love. The liveness of this episode, coupled with the surveillant aspect, adds to the spectacle and authenticates her failure.

Perhaps the lesson to take from the BI is that a woman in search of love had better be sure to never appear as most of the women do on these shows. What the long list of paradoxes and contradictions also reveals is that change is never good, consistency is always good. The most important message the BI has for women is that the best stance to find love is to be content with exactly who we are, to always be the same, and to be proud of this sameness. This suggests a need for intense self-monitoring and self-discipline—either that, or that women are ideally very simple creatures, remaining timelessly exactly the same in every conceivable social sphere.

Finally, most importantly, this book emphasizes that the BI tells particular stories from among a multiplicity of stories that could be told from the endless miles of footage shot. These are mediate stories. The BI tells its stories about women with the help of specific mechanisms and a particular logic that makes sense because of the situated context. While one of the tasks of this book is to decipher why a particular story about women failing at love is being told at this particular time and in this manner, we might also ask, in a more general sense using the framework I have outlined, how other stories get told. How do stories "make sense"? What logic is used to tell a particular story? What are the mechanisms used to tell a story? How might an examination of the mechanisms and the logic of a story help us understand the imperatives of that story? It is my hope that the questions posed in this work, the way the questions have been posed, and the ways in which I tried to answer these questions can be directed at other happenings in our culture.

Notes

1.   For a more detailed discussion of neo-liberalism, see Hay (2003), Ouellette (2004), Ouellette and Hay (2008), and Rose (1996).

2.   Implicit is the fact that this woman has ceded control over her presentation of self by allowing others (the producers of the series) to formulate an image of who she is. Her task is then to claim that this produced image is who she is, at all times, across all social spheres.

Bibliography

Adalian, J. (February 11, 2009). ABC's 'Bachelor' set for re-up after ratings bounce. *TV Week, 2*. Retrieved from www.tvweek.com/news/2009/02/bachelors_ surprising_ ratings_b.php.

Ahmed, L. (1982). Western ethnocentrism and perceptions of the harem. *Feminist Studies, 8*(3), 521-534.

Alloula, M. (1986). *The colonial harem*. Minneapolis: University of Minnesota Press.

Andrejevic, M. (2002). The kinder, gentler gaze of Big Brother. *New Media and Society, 4*, 251-270.

Andrejevic, M. (2004). *Reality TV: The work of being watched*. New York: Rowman & Littlefield Publishers, Inc.

Aparicio, F., Chávez-Silverman, R., and Chávez-Silverman, S. (1997). *Tropicalizations: Transcultural representations of Latinidad*. Hanover, NH: University Press of New England.

Appadurai, A. (1996). Diversity and disciplinarity as cultural artifacts. In C. Nelson and D. P. Gaonkar (Eds.), *Disciplinarity and Dissent in cultural studies* (pp. 23-36). New York: Routledge.

Arthurs, J. (2003). *Sex and the City* and consumer culture: Remediating postfeminist drama. *Feminist Media Studies, 3*(1), 83-98.

Azote, A. (2006). Heart, be still: ABC's "Bachelor" revives. *Media Life*. Retrieved from http://www.medialifemagazine.com/artman2/publish/Television_44/Heart_be_still_ ABC_s_Bachelor_revives_3309.asp.

Bellah, R. N., Madsen, R., Sullivan, W. M., Swindler, A., and Tipton, A. M. (1996). *Habits of the heart: Individualism and commitment in American life*. Los Angeles: University of California Press.

Bennett, T. (2003). Culture and governmentality. In J. Z. Bratich, J. Packer, and C. McCarthy (Eds.), *Foucault, cultural studies, and governmentality* (pp. 47-66). Albany: State University of New York Press.

Ben-Yehuda, N. (1990). *The politics and morality of deviance: Moral panics, drug abuse, deviant science and reversed stigmatization.* Albany: State University of New York Press.

Berger, J. (1977). *Ways of seeing.* London: Penguin Books.

Brooks, A. (1997). *Postfeminisms: Feminism, cultural theory, and cultural forms.* New York: Routledge.

Boylorn, Robin M. (2008). As seen on TV: An autoethnographic reflection on race and reality television. *Critical Studies in Media Communication,* 25(4), 413-433.

Cancian, F. M. (1987). *Love in America: Gender and self-development.* Cambridge: Cambridge University Press.

Chodorow, N. (1978). *The reproduction of mothering: Psychoanalysis and the sociology of gender.* Berkeley: University of California Press.

Chung Simpson, C. (1998). Out of an obscure place: Japanese war brides and cultural pluralism in the 1950s. *differences: A Journal of Feminist Cultural Studies,* 10(3), 47-81.

Cloud, D. (2010). The irony bribe and reality television: Investment and detachment in *The Bachelor. Critical Studies in Media Communication,* 27(5), 413-437.

Cloud, D. L. (1998). *Control and consolation in American culture and politics: Rhetoric of therapy.* London: Sage Publications.

Cloud, D. L. (1996). Hegemony or concordance? The rhetoric of tokenism in 'Oprah' Winfrey's rags-to-riches biography. *Critical Studies in Mass Communication,* 13, 115-37.

Clissold, B. D. (2004). *Candid Camera* and the origins of reality TV. In S. Holmes and D. Jermyn (Eds.), *Understanding reality television* (pp. 33-53). London: Routledge.

Collins, S. (2002, December 4). Music specials mostly flat as sweep goes out quietly. *Hollywood Reporter,* pp. 4, 31.

Collins, S. (2002, November 6). Super sophs boost flagging nets. *Hollywood Reporter,* pp. 4, 27.

Collins, S. (2002, October 11-13). For nets, it's midweek mayhem. *Hollywood Reporter,* pp. 1, 65

Couldry, N. (2002). Playing for celebrity: *Big Brother* as ritual event. *Television and New Media,* 3, 284-291.

Cruikshank, B. (1996). Revolutions within: Self-government and self-esteem. In A. Barry, T. Osborne, and N. Rose (Eds.), *Foucault and political reason: Liberalism, neoliberalism, and rationalities of government* (pp. 231-252). Chicago: Chicago University Press.

Cushman, P. (1995). *Constructing the self, constructing America: A cultural history of psychotherapy.* Boston: Addison-Wesley Publications.

DeFranciso, V. L., and O'Connor, P. (1995). A feminist critique of self-help books on heterosexual romance: Read'em and weep. *Women's Studies in Communication,* 18, 217-227.

De Moraes, L. (2008, May 21). Three rounds, two Davids, one knockout. *The Washington Post.* p. C01.

Dovey, J. (2000). *Freakshow: First person media and factual television.* London: Pluto Press.

Dow, B. J. (1996). *Prime-time feminism: Television, media culture, and the women's movement since 1970.* Philadelphia: University of Pennsylvania Press.

DuBois, P. (1988). *Sowing the body: Psychoanalysis and ancient representations of women.* Chicago: University of Chicago Press.

Dubrofsky, R. E., and Hardy, A. (2008). Performing race in *Flavor of Love* and *The Bachelor*. *Critical Studies in Media Communication*, 25(4), 373-392.

Dubrofsky, R. (2002). *Ally Mcbeal* as postfeminist icon: The aestheticizing and fetischizing of the independent working woman. *Communication Review*, 5(4), 265-284.

Ehrenreich, B., and English, D. (1978). *For her own good: 150 years of expert's advice to women*. New York: Anchor Press.

Eksterowicz, H., and Gioia, G. (2004). *Nobody's perfect: What to do when you've fallen for a jerk but you want to make it work*. New York: CDS Books.

Esposito, J. (2009). What does race have to do with *Ugly Betty*?: An analysis of privilege and postracial(?) representations on a television sitcom. *Television and New Media*, 10(6), 521-535.

Ewing, S. (1999). *All consuming images: The politics of style in contemporary culture*. New York: Basic Books.

Feng Sun, C. (2003). Ling Woo in historical context: The new face of Asian American stereotypes on television. In Gail Dines and Jean M. Humez (Eds), *Gender, race, and class in media: A text-reader, second edition* (pp. 656-664). London: Sage Publications.

Foucault, M. (1988). Technologies of the self. In L. H. Martin, H. Gutman, and P. H. Hutton (Eds.), *Technologies of the self: A seminar with Michel Foucault* (pp. 16-49). Amherst: University of Massachusetts Press.

Foucault, M. (1990). *The history of sexuality: An introduction, volume 1*. New York: Vintage Books.

Foucault, M. (1991). Questions of method: Michel Foucault. In G. Burchell, C. Gordon, and P. Miller (Eds.), *The Foucault effect: Studies in governmentality* (pp. 73-86). Chicago: University of Chicago Press.

Foucault, M. (1995). *Discipline and punish: The birth of the prison*. New York: Vintage Books.

Gamble, S. (1999). *The icon critical dictionary of feminism and postfeminism*. Cambridge: Icon Books.

Gauntlett, D. (2002). Michel Foucault: Discourses and lifestyles. In D. Gauntlett (Ed.), *Media, gender, and identity: An introduction* (pp. 125-144). New York: Routledge.

Gergen, K. J. (1991). *The saturated self: Dilemmas of identity in contemporary life*. New York: Basic Books.

Gilligan, C. (1982). *In a different voice*. London: Harvard University Press.

Goldman, R., Heath, D., and Smith, S. L. (1991). Commodity feminism. *Critical Studies in Mass Communication*, 8, 333-51.

Goodstein, E. (1992). Southern belles and southern buildings: The built environment as text and context in "designing women." *Critical Studies in Mass Communication*, 9(2), 170-185.

Graham, J. (2004, September). Could you be a reality-TV contestant? *Cosmopolitan*, 198-202.

Gray, H. (1991). Television, black Americans, and the American dream. In R. Avery and D. Eason (Eds.), *Critical perspectives in media and society* (pp. 294-306). New York: Guilford Press.

Gray, H. (1995). *Watching race: Television and the struggle for "blackness."* London: University of Minnesota Press.

Grindstaff, L. (2002). *The money shot: Trash, class, and the making of TV talk shows*. Chicago: University of Chicago Press.

Grodin, D. (1991). The interpreting audience: The therapeutics of self-help book reading. *Critical Studies in Mass Communication,* 8, 404-420.

Grossberg, L. (1997). The circulation of cultural studies. In L. Grossberg (Ed.), *Bringing it all back home: Essay on cultural studies* (pp. 234-244). Durham, NC: Duke University Press.

Guiney, R. (2003). *What a difference a year makes: How life's unexpected setbacks can lead to unexpected joy.* Los Angeles: Tarcher/Penguin.

Guzman, M. A and A. N. Valdivia. (2004). Brain, brow, and booty: Latina iconicity in U.S. popular culture. *The Communication Review,* 7(2), 205–221.

Hall, S. (2003). The whites of their eyes. In G. Dines and J. M. Humez (Eds.), *Gender, race, and class in media: A text-reader (2nd ed.)* (pp. 89-93). London: Sage Publications.

Harvey, J. (2006). The amazing 'race': Discovering a true American. In D. S. Escoffery (Ed.), *How real is reality TV?: Essays on representation and truth* (pp. 212-227). Jefferson, NC: McFarland and Company.

Hare-Muslin, R. T. (1997). Discourse in the mirrored room: A postmodern analysis of therapy. In M. M. Gergen and S. N. Davis (Eds.), *Toward a new psychology of gender: A reader* (pp. 553-574). New York: Routledge.

Hasinoff, A. A. (2008). Fashioning race for the free market on *America's Next Top Model. Critical Studies in Media Communication,* 25(3), 324-343.

Hay, J. (2003). Unaided virtues: The (neo)liberalization of the domestic sphere and the new architecture of community. In J. Z. Bratich, J. Packer, and C. McCarthy (Eds.), *Foucault, cultural studies and governmentality* (pp. 165-206). New York: State University Press of New York.

Helford, E. R. (2000). Postfeminism and the female action-adventure hero: Positioning *Tank Girl.* In M. S. Barr (Ed.), *Future females, the next generation* (pp. 291-308). Lanham, MD: Rowman & Littlefield.

hooks, b. (1992). Madonna: Plantation mistress or soul sister? In b. hooks (Ed.), *Black looks: Race and representation* (pp. 157-164). Toronto, ON: Between the Lines.

Hyun Yi Kang, L. (2002). *Compositional subjects: Enfiguring Asian/American women.* Durham, NC: Duke University Press.

Illouz, E. (1991). Reason within passion: Love in women's magazines. *Critical Studies in Mass Communication,* 8, 231-248.

Jhally, S. (director). (1995). *Dreamworlds 2: Desire, sex, power in music video.* [Videotape]. Northampton, MA: Media Education Foundation.

Jones, A. (1994). Postfeminism, feminist pleasures, and embodied theories of art. In J. Frueh, C. L. Langer, and A. Raven (Eds.), *New feminist criticism: Art, identity, action* (pp. 16-41). New York: IconEditions.

Jones, A. (1992). Feminism incorporated: Reading "postfeminism" in an anti-feminist age. *Afterimage,* 2(5), 10-15.

Jones, J. M. (2003). Show your real face. *New Media and Society,* 5(3), 400-421.

Joyrich, L. (1992). All that television allows: TV melodrama, postmodernism and consumer culture. In L. Spigel and D. Mann (Eds.), *Private screenings* (pp. 227-251). Minneapolis: University of Minnesota Press.

Kaminer, W. (1992). *I'm dysfunctional, you're dysfunctional: The recovery movement and other self-help fashions.* New York: Addison-Wesley Publishing Company, Inc.

Katz, A. H. (1993). *Self-help in America: A social movement perspective.* New York: Twayne.

Kaufman, A. (July 28, 2009). The Bachelorette's attractive match. *Los Angeles Times.* Retrieved from http://latimesblogs.latimes.com/showtracker/2009/07/the-bachelorettes-attractive-match.html.

Kendall, G., and Wickham, G. (2001). Ordering through routinisation: Technique, technology and self. In G. Kendall and G. Wickham (Eds.), *Understanding culture: Cultural studies, order, ordering* (pp. 149-160). London: Sage.

Kilbourne, J. (1999). *Can't buy my love: How advertising changes the way we think and feel.* New York: Simon & Schuster.

Kim, L. S. (2001). Sex and the single girl in postfeminism. *Television and New Media,* 2(4), 319-334.

King, G. (2005). Just like a movie? 9/11 and Hollywood spectacle. In G. King (Ed.), *The spectacle of the real: From Hollywood to "reality" TV and beyond* (pp. 47-58). Bristol, UK: Intellect.

Kraszewski, J. (2004). Country hicks and urban cliques: Mediating race, reality, and liberalism on MTV's *The Real World.* In S. Murray and L. Ouellette (Eds.), *Reality TV: Remaking television culture* (pp. 179-196). New York: New York University Press.

Lasch, C. (1979). *The culture of narcissism.* New York: W.W. Norton and Company Inc.

Lasch, C. (1984). *The minimal self: Psychic survival in troubled times.* New York: W.W. Norton.

Lears, T. J. (1983). From salvation to self-realization; Advertising at the therapeutic roots of consumer culture. In R. W. Fox and T. J. Lears (Eds.), *The culture of consumption: Critical essays in American history* (pp. 1-38). New York: Pantheon.

Levin, G. (2007, November 28). No rose is good news. *USA Today,* p. 3D.

Lisotta, C. (2005, April 18). Is honeymoon over for ABC's "Bachelor"? *Broadcasting and Cable,* pp. 11, 24, 16.

López, A. M. (1991). Are all Latinas from Manhattan?: Hollywood, ethnography, and cultural colonialism. In L. D. Friedman (Ed.), *Unspeakable images: Ethnicity and the American cinema* (pp. 404-424). Chicago: University of Illinois Press.

Lotz, A. D. (2001). Postfeminist television criticism: Rehabilitating critical terms and identifying postfeminist attributes. *Feminist Media Studies,* 1(1), 105-121.

Lubiano, W. (1997). *The house that race built: Black Americans, U.S. terrain.* New York: Pantheon Books.

Lyne, A. (1987). *Fatal Attraction.* United States. Paramount Pictures.

Mann, P. (1997). Musing as a feminist in a postfeminist era. In J. Dean (Ed.), *Feminism and the new democracy* (pp. 222-243). London: Sage.

Maynard, J. (2007, May 31). Idol lets fox pull victory from the jaws of defeat. *The Washington Post,* p. C07.

McChesney, R. W. (1999). *Rich media, poor democracy: Communication politics in dubious times.* New York: The New Press.

McClintock, A. (1993). Gonad the barbarian and the Venus flytrap: Portraying the female and male orgasm. In L. Segal and M. McIntosh (Eds.), *Sex exposed: Sexuality and the pornography debate* (pp. 111-131). Piscataway, NJ: Rutgers University Press.

Mika, K. (March 10, 2010). ABC prime-time ratings results for the week of March 1-7, 2010. *Entertainment Beacon.* Retrieved from http://www.entertainmentbeacon.com/news/television/4614-abc-prime-time-ratings-results-for-the-week-of-march-1-7-2010.

Moseley, R., and Read, J. (2002). Having it ally: Popular television post-feminism. *Feminist Media Studies,* 2(2), 231-249.

Mulvey, L. ([1975] 1992). Visual pleasure and narrative cinema. In J. Caughie, A. Kuhn, and M. Merck (Eds.), *The sexual subject: A screen reader in sexuality* (pp. 22-34). London: Routledge.

Murray, S., and Ouellette, L. (2009). Introduction. In S. Murray and L. Ouellette (Eds.), *Reality TV: Remaking television culture (2nd ed.)* (pp. 1-22). New York: New York University Press.

Nakayama, T. K., and Krizek, R. L. (1999). Whiteness as a strategic rhetoric. In T. K. Nakayama and J. N. Martin (Eds.), *Whiteness: The communication of social identity* (pp. 87-106). Thousand Oaks, CA: Sage.

Negrón-Mutaner, F. (1997). Jennifer's butt. *Aztlán*, 22(2), 181-194.

Newman, K. (2000). The problem that has a name: *Ally McBeal* and the future of feminism. *Colby Quarterly*, 36(4), 262-265.

Ono, K. A., (2009). *Contemporary media culture and the remnants of a colonial past.* New York: Peter Lang.

Ono, K. A. (2008). The biracial subject as passive receptacle for Japanese American memory in come see the paradise. In M. Beltran and C. Fojas (Eds.), *Mixed race Hollywood* (pp. 136-156). New York: New York University Press.

Ono, K. A. (2000). To be a vampire on Buffy the Vampire Slayer: Race and other socially marginalizing positions on horror TV. In E. R. Helford (Ed.), *Fantasy girls: Gender in the new universe of science fiction and fantasy television* (pp. 163-186). New York: Rowman & Littlefield Publishers, Inc.

Ono, K. A., and V. N. Pham. (2008). *Asian Americans and the media.* Malden, MA: Polity Press.

Ono, K. A., and Sloop, J. M. (2002). *Shifting borders: Rhetoric, immigration, and California's proposition 187.* Philadelphia: Temple University Press.

Orbe, M. P. (Ed.). (2008). Special issue of race in reality TV. *Critical Studies in Media Communication*, 25(4).

Osajima, K. (2005). Asian Americans as the model minority: An analysis of the popular press images in the 1960s and 1980s. In K. A. Ono (Ed.), *Blackwell companion to Asian American studies* (pp. 215-225). Malden, MA: Blackwell Publishing Ltd.

Ouellette, L. (2002). Victims no more: Postfeminism, television, and Ally McBeal. *Communication Review*, 5(4), 315-335.

Ouellette, L. (2004). Take responsibility for yourself: Judge Judy and the neoliberal citizen. In S. Murray and L. Ouellette (Eds.), *Reality TV: Remaking television culture* (pp. 40-56). New York: New York University Press.

Ouellette, L. and Hay, J. (2008). *Better living through reality TV: Television and post-welfare citizenship.* Malden, MA: Blackwell.

Owen, A. S., Stein, S. R., and Vande Berg, L. R. (2007). Leaving the mothership: Postmodernism and postfeminism in Ally McBeal and Sex and the City. Bad girls: Cultural politics and media representations of transgressive women (pp. 91-133). New York: Peter Lang

Patsuris, P. (2004, September 7). The most profitable reality TV shows. *Forbes.* Retrieved from www.forbes.com/home/business/2004/09/07/cx_pp_0907reality tv.html.

Paulsen, W. (2003, October 31). Are two less than one?: The next Joe Millionaire bombs on back-to-back nights. *Reality TV World.* Retrieved from www.realitytvworld .com/index/articles/story.php?s=1925.

Payne, D. (1989). *Coping with failure: The therapeutic uses of rhetoric.* Columbia: University of South Carolina Press.

Peck, J. (1995). TV talk shows as therapeutic discourse: The ideological labor of the televised talking cure. *Communication Theory*, 5(1), 58-81.

Pecora, V. P. (2002). The culture of surveillance. *Qualitative Sociology*, 25, 345-358.

Poster, M. (1984). *Foucault, Marxism and history: Mode of production versus mode of information*. Cambridge, MA: Polity Press.

Probyn, E. (1993). Choosing choice: Images of sexuality and "choiceoisie" in popular culture. In S. Fisher and K. Davis (Eds.), *Negotiating at the margins: The gendered discourses of power and resistance*. Piscataway, NJ: Rutgers University Press.

Probyn, E. (1997). New traditionalism and post-feminism: TV does the home. In C. Brunsdon, J. D'Acci, and L. Spigel (Eds.), *Feminist television criticism* (pp. 126-138). Oxford: Clarendon Press.

Projansky, S., and Ono, K. A. (1999). Strategic whiteness as cinematic racial politics. In T. K. Nakayama and J. Martin (Eds.), *Whiteness: The communication of social identity* (pp. 149-176). Newbury Park, CA: Sage.

Projansky, S. (2001). *Watching rape*. New York: New York University Press.

Radway, J. (1984). *Reading the romance: Women, patriarchy and popular literature*. Chapel Hill: The University of North Carolina Press.

Rapping, E. (1996). *The culture of recovery: Making sense of the recovery movement in women's lives*. Boston: Beacon Press.

Richmond, R. (2002, July 8). Unscripted TV: Real, or really phony? *Hollywood Reporter*, pp. 1, 21, 25.

Ricoeur, P. (1978). *The philosophy of Paul Ricoeur*. Boston: Beacon Press.

Riessman, F., and Carroll, D. (1995). *Redefining self-help: Policy and Practice*. San Francisco: Jossey-Bass Publishers.

Rimke, H. M. (2000). Governing citizens through self-help literature. *Cultural Studies*, 14(1), 61-78.

Robertson, C. (2009). A documentary regime of verification. *Cultural Studies*, 23 (3), 1-26.

Robertson, C. (2006). A ritual of verification?: The nation, the state and the U.S. passport. In J. Packer and C. Robertson (Eds.), *Thinking with James Carey: Essays on communications, transportation, history* (pp. 177-198). New York: Peter Lang.

Robins, M. J. (2003, January 25-31). 'The Bachelor: Officer and a gentleman' ends with a ratings bang, The Robins Report. *TV Guide*, pp. 53-55.

Rogers, S. (2004, April 28). ABC orders two more "The Bachelor" installments for 2004-05 schedule. Retrieved from www.realitytvworld.com/index/articles/story .php?s=2525.

Rogers, S. (2003, December 13). Ratings: Trista and Ryan's wedding finale dominates timeslot, draws over 17 million viewers. *Reality TV World*. Retrieved from http://www.realitytvworld.com/index/articles/story.php?s=2090.

Rogers, S. (2003, October 22). Survivor takes a ratings hit from Bachelor special, places second behind Friends. *Reality TV World*. Retrieved from www.realitytvworld .com/index/articles/story.php?s=2020.

Rogers, S. (2006, November 17). Report: ABC greenlights production of a tenth The Bachelor edition. *Reality TV World*. Retrieved from www.realitytvworld.com /news/report-abc-greenlights-production-of-tenth-the-bachelor-edition-4423.php.

Rose, N. (1996). Governing advanced liberal democracies. In A. Barry, T. Osborne, and N. Rose (Eds.), *Foucault and political reason: Liberalism, neoliberalism, and rationalities of government* (pp. 37-64). Chicago: Chicago University Press.

Rowe, K. K. (1997). Roseanne: Unruly woman as domestic goddess. In C. Brunsdon, J. D'Acci, and L. Spigel (Eds.), *Feminist television criticism* (pp. 74-83). Oxford: Clarendon Press.

Ruiz, M. V. (2002). Border narratives, HIV/Aids, and Latina/o health in the United States: A cultural analysis. *Feminist Media Studies, 2*(1), 37-62.

Saade, J. and Borgenicht, J. (2004). *The reality TV handbook: An insider's guide.* Philadelphia: Quirk Books.

Said, E. W. (1978). *Orientalism.* New York: Vintage Books.

Seidman, R. (July 20, 2010). ABC's 'The Bachelorette' draws most-watched telecast since February 2004 excluding finales. *TV By the Numbers.* Retrieved from http://tvbythenumbers.com/2010/07/20/abcs-the-bachelorette-draws-most-watched-telecast-since-february-2004-excluding-finales/57709.

Schiller, D. (1999). *Digital capitalism: Networking the global market system.* Cambridge, MA: MIT Press.

Schilling, K. M., and Fuehrer, A. (1993). The politics of women's self-help books. *Feminism and Psychology, 3,* 418-422.

Schreiber, F. R. (1973). *Sybil.* New York: Warner Books.

Shaheen, J. G. (2001). *Reel bad Arabs: How Hollywood vilifies a people.* New York: Olive Branch Press.

Shattuc, J. M. (1997). *The talking cure: TV talk shows and women.* New York: Routledge.

Shohat, E., and Stam, R. (1994). *Unthinking Eurocentrism: Multiculturalism and the media.* New York: Routledge.

Shohat, E. (1991). Ethnicities-in-relation: Toward a multicultural reading of American cinema. In L. D. Friedman (Ed.), *Unspeakable images: Ethnicity and the American cinema* (pp. 215-250). Chicago: University of Illinois Press.

Simonds, W. (1992). *Women and self-help culture: Reading between the lines.* Piscatawy, NJ: Rutgers University Press.

Simonds, W. (1996). All consuming selves: Self-help literature and women's identities. In D. Grodin, and T. R. Lindlof (Eds.), *Constructing the self in a mediated world* (pp. 15-29). Thousand Oakes, CA: Sage Publications Inc.

Stacey, J. (1987). Sexism by a subtler name: Postindustrial conditions and postfeminist consciousness in the Silicon Valley. *Socialist Review, 17* (6), 7-28.

Stallybrass, P., and White, A. (1986). *Transgression: The politics and poetics of transgression.* Ithaca, NY: Cornell University Press.

Stam, R. (1991). Bakhtin, polyphony, and ethnic/racial representation. In L. D. Friedman (Ed.), *Unspeakable images: Ethnicity and the American cinema* (pp. 251-276). Chicago: University of Illinois Press.

Starker, S. (1989). *Oracle at the supermarket: The American preoccupation with self-help books.* New Brunswick, N.J.: Transaction.

The Bachelor (television series). (2002-2010). ABC.

The Bachelorette (television series). (2003-2010). ABC.

Tincknell, E., and Raghuram, P. (2002). Big brother: Reconfiguring the active audience of cultural studies? *European Journal of Cultural Studies, 5,* 199-215.

Toff, B. (2008, July 9). ABC takes Monday. *The New York Times,* p. 2.

TV Guide. (2002, September 7-13). Radnor, PA: Triangle Publications. p. 36.

Valdivia, A. (2005). Geographies of Latinidad: Deployments of radical hybridity in the mainstream. In C. McCarthy, W. Crichlow, and G. Dimitriadis (Eds.), *Race, identity, and representation in education (Critical social thought)* (pp. 307-320). New York: Routledge.

Valdivia, A. N. (2000). *A Latina in the land of Hollywood: And other essays on media culture.* Tucson: University of Arizona Press.

Wallace, M. (1990). *Invisibility blues: From pop to theory.* New York: Verso.

Walters, S. D. (1995). *Material girls: Making sense of feminist cultural theory.* Berkeley: University of California Press.

Wang, G. (2010). A shot at half-exposure: Asian Americans in reality TV shows. *Television and New Media*, 11(5), 404-427.

Wasko, J. (2002). *Understanding Disney: The manufacture of fantasy.* Cambridge, UK: Polity Press.

White, M. (1992). *Tele-advising: Therapeutic discourse in American television.* Chapel Hill: The University of North Carolina Press.

White, M. (2002). Television, therapy, and the social subject: Or, the TV therapy machine. In J. Friedman (Ed.), *Reality squared: Televisual discourse on the real* (pp. 313-322). Piscataway, NJ: Rutgers University Press.

Williams, L. (1989). *Hard core: Power, pleasure and the frenzy of the visible.* Berkeley: University of California Press.

Williams, L. (1993). Pornographies on/scene or diff'rent strokes for diff'rent folks. In L. Segal and M. McIntosh (Eds.), *Sex exposed: Sexuality and the pornography debate* (pp. 233-265). Piscataway, NJ: Rutgers University Press.

Yep, G, and Camacho, A. (2004). The normalization of heterogendered relations in The Bachelor. *Feminist Media Studies*, 4(3), 338-341.

Yuval-Davis, N. (2000). *Gender and nation.* Thousand Oaks, CA: Sage.

Index

About the Author

Dr. Rachel E. Dubrofsky is an Assistant Professor in the Department of Communication at the University of South Florida and received her Ph.D. from the Institute of Communications Research at the University of Illinois, Urbana-Champaign. Her research interests include television and media studies, critical cultural studies, surveillance, digital culture, race, gender, and space. She has published articles in *Television and New Media, Critical Studies in Media Communication,* and *Communication Theory.* Her current projects look at the reality TV phenomena and online social networking sites.